WITHDRAWN
UTSA LIBRARIES

The People in Your Life

The People in Your Life

PSYCHIATRY

AND PERSONAL RELATIONS

BY TEN LEADING AUTHORITIES

PREPARED UNDER THE AUSPICES OF TOWN HALL, NEW YORK
EDITED BY MARGARET M. HUGHES
WITH A FOREWORD BY
ISABEL LEIGHTON

Essay Index Reprint Series

 BOOKS FOR LIBRARIES PRESS
FREEPORT, NEW YORK

Copyright 1951 by Alfred A. Knopf, Inc.

Reprinted 1971 by arrangement

INTERNATIONAL STANDARD BOOK NUMBER:
0-8369-2204-2

LIBRARY OF CONGRESS CATALOG CARD NUMBER:
71-142706

PRINTED IN THE UNITED STATES OF AMERICA

FOREWORD

About the time the embattled disciples of Dr. Sigmund Freud were struggling for even a token acceptance of his psychiatric theories, a stonemason must have been perched above the entrance to Town Hall of New York chipping out the words: "Ye shall know the truth, and the truth shall make you free." Since then Town Hall has devoted itself to the stimulation of a lively interest in the truth about many things. It has never run from controversy. It has, in fact, encouraged it, thinking to flick the imaginations of men and women into wider flights, seeking through the dissemination of knowledge to light one way to wisdom.

With the creation of the National Mental Health Act in 1946, Town Hall became aware, through the revealing testimony that ensured its passage, of the need not only for the elements the bill provided but for a positive public approach toward mental health. Mental health, Town Hall realized, was something to attain. It was not merely something to repair when the human emotional machinery broke down.

Not long after the bill became a reality, Town Hall plotted its initial psychiatric course. It reached out toward *leading dedicated minds* practicing in the field and found them enthusiastic about enlisting appropriate lay interest in psychiatry. Out of this collaboration between therapists and Town Hall, six lectures were scheduled. The participating doctors were: Dr. Carl Binger, Dr. Edward A. Strecker, Dr. Franz Alexander, Dr. Roy R. Grinker, Dr. Thomas A. C. Rennie, and Dr. Frank Fremont-Smith.

There was no need even then to beat the bushes for an audience. With half the nation's hospital beds occupied by mentally disturbed patients, avid listeners to reputable men abounded among the families and friends of people to whom, unhappily, the subject was of more than academic interest. There were also large numbers of objectively interested subscribers. There were, additionally, teachers, social workers, trained nurses, medical students, occupational therapists, and clergymen, most of them seeking to enlarge their skills.

That hour and a half on six successive Mondays in the late afternoon was time profitably spent. The sessions were stimulating, informative, and valid. Misconceptions took wings, taboos were broken down. To many who had never had traffic with one before, the *psychiatrist* emerged as an M.D. and not a witch doctor.

Yielding far from reluctantly to public pressure, Town Hall set up another series of talks the following season, consisting, this time, of eight sessions. The participating lecturers were again leading figures in the psychiatric arena: Dr. Thomas A. C. Rennie, Dr. Milton J. E. Senn, Dr. Kenneth E. Appel, Dr. Edward Strecker, Dr. Howard A. Rusk, Dr. Margaret Mead, Dr. Robert P. Knight, and Dr. Carl Binger. The original formula of an hour's lecture followed by half an hour of questions and answers remained. So did the somewhat haphazard technique of choosing subject matter purely for its own sake rather than relating it to a central theme in the interest of achieving a well-rounded entity.

It was not until the third series came into being—the series that comprises this book—that the program could properly be said to have achieved definite and potent form. Recognizing that it was not enough to offer a group of talks each of which had something to say for itself, Town Hall attempted to create a concept built around a theme. This tenuous thread

Foreword [vii

was therefore woven through the program and, it is to be hoped, created the unifying force that was felt to be essential if the series was to justify its existence.

The ten chapters that follow deal with ten of the relationships that at some time in every life are its warp and woof. One is by no means assuming that other vital relationships do not play a sturdy part in the course of a lifetime; but these are, perhaps, the obvious ones, the ones most commonly shared by people knowing varying kinds of distress. There are very few among us, if any, who are not frequently prey to many confusions, who are not assailed by deep despair, who do not often question their capacity to deal adequately with the problems that light on their horizons.

It is only honest to say at the outset that these pages contain no automatic blueprint for happiness, no jerry-built solutions to self-doubts, no pat, ready answers to the insistent questions that plague us all. They do, however, contribute much to self-understanding. They foster a wider acceptance of appropriate personal frailty. By awakening a perhaps hitherto slumbering awareness of undiscovered capacities, they change the signpost on many a path of life from "Danger Ahead" to "Under Construction."

Surcease from besetting worries is not promised the reader. No anesthetic oblivion is inherent in lines to come. The reader may, in fact, discover new problems he had not realized needed facing; but if the problems are posed, many of the tools with which to grapple with them are put into his hands. The use to which he puts them lies largely within his needs and his determination to make them his own.

If there is a handbook to easy living, this is not it; nor is each piece in this collection intended as a definitive work on the subject it undertakes to discuss. Not this book nor any other can be all things to all men. In it, however, there is something for everyone. It may not eliminate mental roadblocks but it gives ample evidence of the existence of detours that are passable.

Town Hall takes this opportunity of expressing its profound gratitude to the men and women who peopled these programs. Additionally, as co-ordinator of these several courses, I want much to record my deep personal appreciation for many things. I shall never cease to be most happily in the debt of two great friends, Mary Woodard Lasker, who introduced me to psychiatry, and Dr. Carl Binger, whose wisdom made it impossible for me to forget it.

ISABEL LEIGHTON

CONTENTS

		PAGE	
FOREWORD *by Isabel Leighton*			V
I	MAN — WOMAN *by Eric Fromm, Ph.D.*		3
II	HUSBAND — WIFE *by Lawrence S. Kubie, M.D.*		28
III	PARENT — CHILD *by Frederick H. Allen, M.D.*		64
IV	AGE — YOUTH *by Francis J. Braceland, M.D.*		93
V	RACE MAJORITY — RACE MINORITY *by Margaret Mead, Ph.D.*		120
VI	STUDENT — TEACHER *by Clyde Kluckhohn, Ph.D.*		158
VII	FRIEND — FRIEND *by John A. P. Millet, M.D.*		182
VIII	EMPLOYER — EMPLOYEE *by Leo H. Bartemeier, M.D.*		209
IX	PASTOR — PARISHIONER *by Rev. Otis R. Rice*		228
X	CITIZEN — COMMUNITY *by George S. Stevenson, M.D.*		249

The People in Your Life

I
MAN — WOMAN
by ERIC FROMM, PH.D.[1]

THE PROBLEM of the relationship between men and women is obviously exceedingly difficult, for if it were not, people wouldn't be mismanaging it as frequently as they do. So the best thing to do in discussing it is to try to raise some questions. If through these questions I can provoke your own thinking, perhaps you will be able to give some answers from your experience.

The first question I want to raise is: does not the topic itself imply a fallacy? It seems to imply that the difficulties in the relationship between man and woman are essentially due to the difference in sex. That is not so. The relationship between man and woman—men and women—is essentially a relationship between human beings. Whatever is good in the relationship between one human being and another is good in the relationship between men and women, and whatever is bad in human relationships is bad in the relationship between men and women.

The particular defects in the relationship between men and women are largely not specific to their male

[1] University of Heidelberg. Fellow of the Washington School of Psychiatry; member of the faculty of Bennington College; chairman of the faculty of William Alanson White Institute of Psychiatry.

and female characteristics, but to their person-to-person human relationships.

I shall come back to this problem a little later, but I want to make a second qualification of this whole topic. The relationship between men and women is a relationship between a victorious and a defeated group. This may sound strange and funny in the United States in the year 1949; yet we have to consider the history of the relationship between men and women in the last five thousand years to understand how history colors the present-day situation and the present-day attitude between the sexes and what they know and feel about each other. Only then can we approach the question of how, specifically, men and women differ; only then can we determine what is characteristic of the relationship between men and women and what is a problem in its own right and not a problem merely of human relationships.

Let me start out with this second question, defining the relationship between men and women as the relationship between a victorious and a defeated group. I said it sounds funny to say this in the United States at this day and age because quite obviously women, certainly in the big cities, don't look and don't feel and don't act like a defeated group.

There has been a good deal of discussion, and not without reason, as to which is the stronger sex in our urban culture today. I do not think the problem is as simple as all that, however. It isn't even as simple as the statement that in America women have accomplished their emancipation and therefore are on equal footing with men makes it appear. I think the struggle of many thousands of years still shows in the particu-

I. Man — Woman

lar way in which the relationship between men and women in our culture is maintained.

There is some good evidence for assuming that the patriarchal society as it existed in China, in India, and in Europe and America for the last five thousand to six thousand years is not the only form in which the two sexes have organized their lives. There is a good deal of evidence that (if not everywhere, at any rate in many places) the patriarchal societies dominated by men were preceded by matriarchal societies. These were characterized by the fact that the woman and mother was the center of society and of the family.

Woman was dominant in the social system and in the family system, and you can see the traces of her dominance in the various religious systems. You find the traces of this old organization even in a document with which we all are familiar, the Old Testament.

If you read the story of Adam and Eve with some objectivity, what do you find? You find that a curse is pronounced against Eve; and indirectly against Adam, because to dominate others is not better than to be dominated. As a punishment for her sin, man shall rule over her, and her desire shall be to her husband.

It is obvious that if the domination of men over women is established as a *new* principle, there must have been a time when this was not so, and indeed we have documents which show that this was the case. If you compare the Babylonian account of the creation with the Biblical story you find that in this Babylonian story, which antecedes the Biblical story in time, something quite different existed. In the center of the Babylonian account you find not a masculine god but a goddess, Tiamat. Her sons tried to rebel against her and eventually defeated her and established the rule of male gods under the leadership of Marduk, the great Babylonian god.

Marduk had to undergo a test of his power in order to prove that he was fit to win the war against the goddess. He had to show that by the power of his word he could destroy a piece of cloth and make it reappear again. This seems like a somewhat silly test, perhaps, and yet it touched essentials, because in a matriarchal society women were clearly superior to men in one respect: they could bear children; the men couldn't. The attempt of men to dethrone the women was connected with their claim that they too could create things and destroy things—not in the natural way in which women could, but by the word and by the spirit.

If you read the Biblical story of creation you will find that it begins where the Babylonian story ends. God creates the world by his word; and in order to emphasize the superiority of patriarchal over matriarchal culture, the Bible story tells us that Eve was created from a man rather than that man was born of woman.

The patriarchal culture, the culture in which men appear to be destined to rule over women, to be the stronger sex, has persisted all over the world. In fact, only in small primitive communities today do we find certain remnants of the older matriarchal form. It is only very recently that man's rule over woman has been breaking down.

In a patriarchal society there existed all the typical ideologies and prejudices that a ruling group always develops regarding those whom they rule: women are emotional, they are undisciplined, they are vain, they

I. Man — Woman

are like children, they are not good organizers, and they are not as strong as men—but they are charming.

Yet it is obvious that these ideas about the nature of women which were developed in patriarchal societies are, in some instances, the very opposite of true. Whence the idea that women are more vain than men? I think anyone who studies man can see that if there is anything that can be said about men it is that they are vain. In fact, they hardly do anything without some element of wanting to show off.

Women are far less vain than men are. It is true enough that women are sometimes forced to show some vanity because they either are or were in the position of those who have to seek favors, being the so-called weaker sex; but certainly the legend that women are more vain than men are is disproved by any dispassionate observation.

Take another prejudice: take the idea that men are tougher than women are. Every nurse can tell you that the percentage of men fainting when they get an injection or a blood test is much greater than the percentage of women, that women on the whole are much better able to endure pain which turns men into helpless children and makes them run to mother. Yet men over the centuries, or rather over thousands of years, have succeeded in spreading the idea that they are the stronger and the tougher sex.

Well, there is nothing surprising about that. It is the typical ideology of a group of people who have to prove that they have a right to rule. If you are not in the majority but almost exactly half of the human race, and have claimed for thousands of years that you have a right to rule over the other half, then your ideologies must be plausible in order to convince the other half, and particularly in order to convince yourself.

In the eighteenth and nineteenth centuries the problem of equality between men and women really became acute. A very interesting phenomenon developed during that period—namely, that those who claimed that women should have equal rights with men also claimed that there was no difference between the two sexes psychologically. As the French formulated it, the soul is sexless; there is no psychological difference whatsoever. Those who were against the political and social equality of women emphasized, often very intelligently and subtly, how different women were from men psychologically. Of course the point they came to again and again was that because of the psychological differences women were better off and fulfilled their destiny better if they did not participate in social and political life on an equal footing.

Even up to this day we find a similar attitude among many feminists, progressives, liberals, or any group who are in favor of equality between human beings in general and between the two sexes specifically; those of this attitude claim that there are no differences, or minimize these differences. They say that whatever differences exist, they are due only to cultural environment and to education, and that there are no intrinsic psychological differences between the sexes that are not the result of such environmental or educational factors.

I am afraid that this viewpoint, which is so popular among the defenders of the equality of men and women, is a bad one in many ways. Perhaps its worst fault is that it isn't true. It is about the same as saying

I. Man — Woman

that there are no psychological differences between various national groups and that anyone who uses the word *race* is then and there saying something terrible. While it may very well be that scientifically the word *race* is not a good word, it is true that there are differences in body and temperament between the peoples of various nations.

The second reason why I think this kind of reasoning is bad is that it suggests false principles. It suggests that equality implies lack of difference, that equality implies that everyone is like everybody else, that equality implies identity. Actually equality and the demand for equality implies the very opposite: namely, that despite all differences no person should be made a tool of the purpose of anyone else, that every human being is an end and purpose in himself or herself. This means that each person is free to develop his or her peculiarity as an individual, as a member of a given sex, as a member of a given nationality. Equality does not imply the negation of difference but the possibility for its fullest realization.

If we imply that equality means that there are no differences, we shall fortify the very tendencies which lead to the impoverishment of our culture—that is, to the "automatization" of individuals and the weakening of that which is the most valuable part of human existence, the unfolding and development of the peculiarities of each person.

In using the word *peculiarities* I should like to remind you how strange a fate this word has had. If we say today that someone is peculiar, we don't mean anything particularly pleasant. Yet this should be the greatest compliment we can pay. Saying that someone is peculiar should mean that he has not given in, that he has retained the most valuable part of human existence, his individuality, that he is a unique person, different from anyone else under the sun.

I think that in America the fallacy of assuming that equality is synonymous with identity is one of the reasons for this peculiar phenomenon in our culture: the differences between the sexes tend to be minimized, tend to be covered up, tend to be argued away. Women try to be like men, men sometimes like women, and the polarity between male and female, between men and women, tends to disappear.

Indeed, I believe that the only answer to the problem, speaking in somewhat general terms, is to work toward a concept of polarity in the relationship between the two sexes. You would not say of the positive or negative pole of an electric current that one is inferior to the other. You would say that the field between them is caused by their polarity, and that this very polarity is the basis of productive forces.

In the same sense the two sexes and that for which they stand (the male and the female aspect in the world, in the universe, and in each of us) are two poles which have to retain their difference, their polarity, in order to exercise the fruitful dynamism, the productive force, that springs from that very polarity.

Let me come now to the second premise, that the relationship between men and women is never better than the relationship between human beings in any given society, and never worse, either. If I were to single out in our interpersonal relations that which most affects and damages relations between men and women, I should speak of what in my book, *Man for*

I. *Man — Woman* [11

Himself, I called the marketing orientation. I should speak of the fact that we all are terribly alone, even though on the surface we are all so social and have "contacts" with so many people.

The average person today is terribly alone and feels alone. He feels himself to be a commodity, by which I mean he feels that his value depends on his success, depends on his salability, depends on approval by others. He feels that it does not depend on the intrinsic or what you might call *use* value of his personality, not on his powers, not on his capacity to love, not on his human qualities—except if he can sell them, except if he can be successful, except if he is approved by others. This is what I mean by the "marketing orientation."

This accounts for the fact that the self-esteem of most people today is very shaky. They do not feel themselves worthy because of their own conviction: "This is me, this is my capacity to love, this is my capacity to think and to feel," but because they are approved by others, because they can sell themselves, because others say: "This is a wonderful man" or "a wonderful woman."

Naturally, when the feeling of self-esteem is dependent upon others it becomes uncertain. Each day is a new battle because each day you have to convince someone, and you have to prove to yourself, that you are all right.

To use an analogy, I would suggest that you consider how handbags would feel on a counter in a store. The handbag of one particular style, of which many have been sold, would feel elated in the evening; and the other handbag, of a style a little out of fashion or a little too expensive or which, for some reason or other, had not been sold, would be depressed.

The one handbag would feel: "I am wonderful," and the other handbag would feel: "I am unworthy," and yet the "wonderful" handbag may not be more beautiful or more useful or have any better intrinsic quality than the other one. The unsold handbag would feel it was not wanted. In our analogy, a handbag's sense of value would depend on its success, on how many purchasers, for one reason or another, preferred the one to the other.

In human terms that means that no one must be peculiar, that one's own personality must be always open to change in order to conform to the latest model. That is why parents often feel embarrassed when they are with their children. The children know the latest model better than the parents do. But the parents are very ready to be taught, to be told, to learn. They, like the children, listen to the latest quotations on the personality market.

And where do you find these market quotations? Where do you read them? In the movies, in the liquor ads, in the clothing ads, in the indications of the ways that important people dress and talk.

A model is considered outmoded after only a few years. I read in the Sunday *Times Magazine* of a little girl of fourteen who said that her mother was so old-fashioned that she still thought it was 1945. At first I didn't understand. I thought it was a misprint until I understood that for this girl 1945 seemed awfully out-of-date. But I am sure her mother knew, nevertheless, that she had to hurry.

I. *Man — Woman* [13

How does this "marketing orientation" affect the relationship between the sexes, between men and women? I think, in the first place, that a great deal of what goes under the name of love is this seeking for success, for approval. One needs someone to tell one not only at four o'clock in the afternoon but also at eight and at ten and at twelve: "You're fine, you're all right, you are doing well." That is one factor.

The other factor is that one also proves one's value by choosing the right person. One needs to be the latest model oneself, but one then has a right also and a duty to fall in love with the latest model. That can be put as crudely as it was put by a boy of eighteen who was asked what the ambition of his life was. He said he wanted to buy a better car; he wanted to change from a Ford to a Buick so that he could pick up a better class of girls.

Well, this boy was at least frank, but I think he expressed something that, in a more subtle way, determines the choice of partners to a large extent in our culture.

The marketing orientation has another effect on the relationship between the sexes. In the marketing orientation everything is patterned, and we are eager to live up to the latest model and to act in the latest way. Accordingly the roles we choose, particularly our sex roles, are highly patterned, but the patterns are not even or uniform. Frequently they are conflicting. Man ought to be aggressive in business and tender at home. He ought to live for his work but not be tired in the evening when he comes home. He ought to be ruthless with his customers or competitors, but he ought to be very honest with his wife and children. He ought to be liked by everyone, and yet he should have the deepest feeling for his family.

Well! The poor man tries to live up to these patterns. Only the fact that he does not take them too seriously probably protects him from going crazy. The same holds true with women. They too have to live patterns that are as contradictory as those for the males.

There always were, of course, in every culture, patterns for what was considered to be male and female, masculine and feminine; but formerly these patterns had at least a certain stability. In a culture in which we depend so much on the *latest* pattern, on being just right, on approval, on fitting in with what is expected, the real qualities that belong to our male or female roles become obscured. Very little specific is left in the relationship between men and women.

If the choices in relationships between men and women are made on the basis of market orientation, of highly patterned roles, one thing must happen: people get bored. I think that the word *bored* does not get the attention it deserves. We speak of all sorts of terrible things that happen to people, but we rarely speak about one of the most terrible things of all: that is, being bored, being bored alone and, worse than that, being bored together.

Many people see only two solutions for this boredom. They avoid being bored by using any of the many avenues our culture offers. They go to parties, make contacts, drink, play cards, listen to the radio, and so kid themselves every day, every evening. Or— and this is partly a matter of to what social class they

I. Man — Woman

belong—they think things are changed by a change of partner. They think this or that marriage was no good because they got the wrong partner, and they suppose that a change of partner will dispel boredom.

People do not see that the main question is not: "Am I loved?" which is to a large extent the question: "Am I approved of? Am I protected? Am I admired?" The main question is: "Can I love?"

That is indeed difficult. To be loved and to "fall in love" is very simple for a while until you get boring and bored. But to love, "to stand in love," as it were, is indeed difficult, although not superhuman; in fact, it is the most essential human quality.

If one cannot be alone with oneself, if one cannot be genuinely interested in others and in oneself, then one cannot be together with anyone else without being bored after a certain time. If the relationship between the sexes becomes a refuge for the loneliness and isolation of the individual, it has very little to do with the potentialities that the real relationship between male and female implies.

There is another fallacy I want to mention. That is the fallacy that the real problem between the sexes is sex. We felt very proud thirty years ago, or many of us did, when during the era of sexual emancipation it seemed that the chains of the past were breaking and that a new phase of human relations between the sexes was opening up. Yet the results were not so wonderful as many thought they would be, because all that glitters isn't sex. There are many motivations for the sexual urge that in themselves are not sexual.

Vanity is one of the greatest stimuli for sex, much more than anything else perhaps; but so is loneliness, so is rebelliousness against an existing relationship. A man who is driven to make new sexual conquests thinks he is motivated by the sexual attraction women have for him, but actually he is motivated by his vanity, by the drive to prove that he is superior to all other males.

No sexual relationship is better than the human relationship between the two people. Sex is very often a short cut to closeness, but it is very deceptive. While sex is certainly an important part of human relationships, it is in our culture so overburdened with all sorts of other functions that I am afraid that what appears as great sexual freedom is by no means exclusively a matter of sex.

Well then, do we know anything about the real differences between men and women? What I have said so far has been negative. If you expected a clear statement of the differences between men and women, you must be disappointed. I don't think we know them. We could not possibly know them in view of the circumstances I mentioned before. If the two sexes have fought for thousands of years, if they have developed prejudices against each other which are characteristic of such fighting situations, how could we possibly at this point know what the real differences are?

Only if we forget about the differences, if we forget about the stereotypes, can we develop a sense of that equality to which each person is an end in himself or herself. Then we might learn something about the differences between men and women.

I should like to mention one difference, however, which I think has a certain relevance to the success of man-woman relationships and so ought to be consid-

I. Man — Woman

ered in our culture. It seems to me that women are probably more capable of being tender than men. This is not surprising, because in woman's relationship to her child tenderness to the child is the main virtue.

It is the fashion today, as you all know, especially if you hear psychiatric lectures, to emphasize that it matters a great deal when the child is weaned, when it is nursed, and how the toilet training proceeds, and people believe their prescriptions for making a child happy by all these little techniques are effective.

What people forget is that there is only one thing that matters, and that is the tenderness of a mother for her child, and tenderness implies a great deal. Tenderness implies love, tenderness implies respect, tenderness implies knowledge. Tenderness, by its very nature, is something quite different from sex or hunger or thirst. You might say, psychologically speaking, that such drives as sex and hunger and thirst are characterized by a self-propelling dynamism, they become more and more intense and end in a rather sudden climax in which satisfaction is achieved and nothing more is wanted, for the moment.

This is the nature of one type of craving or drive. Tenderness belongs to another type of striving. Tenderness is not self-propelling, it has no aim, it has no climax, it has no end. Its satisfaction is in the very act itself, in the joy of being friendly, of being warm, of considering and respecting another person and of making this other person happy.

I have an impression that we have little tenderness in our culture. Take the love stories in the movies. All the passionate kisses are censored out, and yet the audience is supposed to imagine how wonderful they are. The movies allegedly describe passion. They may not be too convincing to many; but to many others this is what is supposed to be love. But how often do you find in the movies an expression of real tenderness between the sexes? or between adults and children? or between human beings in general? I think very seldom. By this I do not mean to say that we do not have the capacity for tenderness, but that tenderness is discouraged in our culture. The reason for this is partly that our culture is one that is purpose-oriented. Everything has a purpose; everything has an aim and should lead somewhere; you must "get somewhere."

It is true enough that we try to save time—then we don't know what we should do with it, so we kill it. But our first impulse is to get somewhere. We have very little feeling for the process of living itself without getting anywhere, just living, just eating or drinking or sleeping or thinking or feeling or seeing something. If living has no purpose, we say, what good is it? Tenderness has no purpose either. Tenderness has not the physiological purpose of relief or sudden satisfaction that sex has. It has no purpose except the enjoyment of a feeling of warmth, pleasure, and care for another person.

So we discourage tenderness. People, especially men, feel uncomfortable when they show tenderness. Furthermore, the very attempt to deny differences between the sexes, the very attempt to make men and women as alike as possible, has prevented women from showing the amount of tenderness of which they are capable and which is specifically feminine.

Here I come back to where I started, to my point that the battle between the sexes is not over. Women

I. Man — Woman

in America have achieved a great deal of equality. This equality is not complete, but it is much more than it used to be. Yet women still have to defend this achievement. Therefore they have to be very eager to prove that they have a right to equality by being as little different as possible from men. And therefore they suppress impulses to tenderness. The result is that men miss tenderness, and as a substitute for it they feel they ought to be admired, and that their self-esteem ought to be validated. So they are in a state of constant dependence and fear; and women are in a state of frustration because they are not allowed to play the role of their own sex with full freedom.

This is certainly an overdrawn picture, and if you say that this is not always so, that it is not fair to insist on it, I would quite agree with you; but, after all, in order to generalize you have to overdraw the picture for the moment.

To conclude these remarks about the relationship between men and women, I would emphasize again that in order to know the difference between them, one must forget about it. One must permit oneself to live fully and spontaneously as a human being and not become preoccupied with the questions: Am I the typical male or the typical female? Do I fit the role prescribed by the culture? Am I successful in my sex role? Only if one forgets such questions, only then will the profound polarity that exists between the sexes and within every human being develop into a productive force.

1. Does your conception of the pure selflessness of tenderness differ from that of Freudian doctrine?

In the first place I didn't mean to imply that tenderness is something selfless. I think tenderness is one of the most self-assertive, joyful experiences anyone can have, and human beings are generally capable of it. For such people there is nothing selfless about it, there is nothing sacrificial about it. It is only sacrificial for the person who cannot be tender.

For a tender, loving mother or a tender person in general it is just as satisfying, makes them just as happy, as the satisfaction of sex, hunger, or any other drive. In Freud's doctrine, to say a word about it, the quality of tenderness unfortunately had very little place. In fact, he hardly talked about it. This is understandable, since his whole work was so centered on the other set of drives, sex and hunger, that tenderness didn't quite have a place in his system.

2. Which is better for the mental health of the population, a patriarchal or a matriarchal society?

This is a futile question, of course, because no one really decides to change things according to what is better for the mental health of the population. There are questions to which the answer is much more definite than that, such as whether it is better for the welfare of people to have no war, to which the answer is definitely yes; and yet we seem to have a very difficult time seeing to it that what we know to be true is practiced.

But whether a matriarchal or patriarchal system is

I. Man — Woman

better is hard to say. In fact, I think the question in this form is wrong because you might say that the matriarchal system emphasizes the elements of natural ties, of natural equality, of love; and the patriarchal system then emphasizes the elements of civilization, of thought, of the state, of invention and industries and, in many ways, of progress, in comparison with the old matriarchal culture.

It seems to me the only answer to your question is that the aim of mankind must be not to have any kind of hierarchy, either matriarchal or patriarchal. We must come to a situation in which the sexes relate to each other without any attempt to dominate. Only in that way can they develop their real differences, their real polarity.

It is important to recognize that our cultural system is not, even though it seems so, the fulfillment of this goal. It is the end of patriarchal domination, but it is not yet a system in which the two sexes meet each other as equals. There is a great deal of fighting going on. I am convinced that this fight is to some extent not simply an individual fight between two people, but is still connected with an age-old fight between the sexes. It is the continuing conflict of a male and a female who are confused and don't quite know what each one's role is. Should he be strong, should she be imaginative, should he be soft, should he run after her, should she do this, should he do that? Over and over men and women pose these questions to themselves. They are confused because we are at the end of a very long-drawn-out battle.

3. Is falling out of love simpler than falling in love? How does a married couple avoid this almost inevitable ending?

That, of course, is a rather dark view, but we have no specific statistics to determine its validity. We have statistics about every other sort of thing, but not on human happiness and not on what goes on in marriage and how happy or unhappy people are. In fact, we have some statistics on happiness too, but they are not particularly enlightening because they are based on the wrong premises. They are based upon the method of merely asking people what they *think* about their happiness. Of course, if you ask "Do you think you are happily married?" of someone who wants to give the answer he thinks is right, he says: "Yes." In fact, he even feels "yes." If you ask a person who is less bound by cliché, he may tell you: "I don't know" or "No." So what you get in these answers is not so much the facts about whether people are happy or unhappy; you get the degree to which they stick to clichés.

To the first part of the question I don't know the answer. I should say it is easy to fall in love, and it is sad to fall out of love. But if I see the question correctly, how falling out of love can be avoided is the point of major concern. It can be avoided only if one does not look at love or at men's and women's relationships as a refuge from an unbearable loneliness. When one does that, one has unrealistic expectations, one makes the other person responsible for something,

I. Man — Woman

one expects something from him that no person could possibly fulfill. Then one is disappointed.

The person who cannot stand on his own, who is in constant need of approval, in constant need of being fathered or mothered, in constant need of being admired, naturally only rarely finds the fulfillment of his expectations; so he gets angry or she gets angry.

I think the only answer to this question of how relations between men and women could be more satisfactory is a richer life for each concerned. If you want to be interesting you have to be interested. If you want to be attractive in the long run, you have to be able to love, you have to be able to care. I can see nothing short of that as the answer to this question.

4. Isn't New York guilty of fostering the emphasis on the commercialized personality by its reverence for the dollar sign?

I don't think uniquely so. I think this is a development we find throughout the world in modern industrialized society. There is no essential difference of principle between various countries or sections of a country, I think. All one can say about New York in this respect is that, being one of the most typical big cities of modern industrial capitalism, it would naturally show certain tendencies more clearly than a small town would.

5. How did you men succeed in overturning the matriarchal society?

I don't know. It is a very good question, but it is always very difficult to understand how any society that seems to be established in power is overthrown. Yet this is the story history tells, that the most powerful societies in one way or another were overthrown.

How? Sometimes by their own inefficiency, by their own inability to organize life. That is probably the main reason why any type of society is overthrown.

I would say that perhaps in this particular case the progress of mankind, the evolution of humanity in the direction of industry, of organization in states, of getting away from primitive agricultural methods—all were factors. That is to say, taking it all together, there was greater emphasis on thought in contradistinction to natural ties, to ties of soil and family. These were the elements in the progressive development of mankind that led to the victory of men.

You might say, to continue this question: what are the elements that today make for overcoming both male and female domination. I don't think anyone has a final answer to that question either; but one answer to it would be that people are unhappy with present-day relationships between the sexes even if they are not too aware of their unhappiness.

It is not a very satisfactory solution, the one we have found. It is fantastically unsatisfactory, in view of all the resources of intellect, education, and material wealth that we have at our disposal, that we have done so poorly with one of the most beautiful possibilities

I. *Man — Woman* [25

the human race has, the relationship between men and women.

6. Is there a psychiatric definition of love, and if so, what is it?

The most beautiful definition of love I know of is to be found in the New Testament. Another beautiful definition I know of is one you will find in the old Testament in the Book of Jonah, and there is another in the prophet Hosea. There are some beautiful definitions of love in Buddhist and Hindu literature. The modern psychiatric definitions of love are not very interesting if you compare them with these very old, traditional definitions of love. It is not the latest definition that is necessarily good. I don't know of any psychiatric definition that would be richer or better than the ones you find in the thinking of those cultures which really were concerned with the question of love.

Perhaps there are some good psychiatric descriptions of what love is *not*—namely, that it is not identical with possessiveness, it is not identical with self-sacrifice, it is not identical with giving oneself up.

Psychiatry might even proceed to say that love is the blending of intense closeness under the condition of complete independence and integrity of two people.

7. If not through new contacts and experiences, how then does one escape boredom?

There are two ways of treating boredom, as there are two ways of treating any other thing. You can treat it symptomatically. If you have a toothache or any other ache, you take something to dull the pain. You can treat it radically, which means going to the roots, literally speaking; that is to say, you try to change the conditions underlying and causing the symptoms. Having more and more contacts, going to parties and what not, is symptomatic treatment. You are not aware of your boredom because you kill it every moment, like taking aspirin every hour of the day; but you just postpone pain and you have to increase your dosage, and sometimes even that doesn't help.

The only other way I know is to investigate what we mean if we speak of new contacts and experiences. That we have met ten new people? That we have made five new friends? New experience. Seen this city and that. Everything on the surface. Everything something new. We hardly know where we have been, as if we were on a cruise or have seen twenty European countries in two weeks. Is that what we mean by new contacts and new experiences? Or do we grow into them? Do we recognize something new? Do we feel more intensely?

You know, it would be a very interesting experiment to find what would happen if people would stay in their room for three days without company, without radio, just with enough food and books, without escape literature, alone for three days. I think you would have thousands of nervous breakdowns after the first day. In fact, I have made the experiment of inquiring of young people how they feel about such a project. Most of them spoke of it as if I were suggesting one of the most dangerous ventures. Going to the North

I. Man — Woman

Pole would be nothing compared to it. They would sleep long and try to dream, and try to take a long time for dressing. Only a very few felt it would be wonderful, three days alone, not disturbed.

Mind you, I am not saying that this ought to be one's life. I am not that misanthropic. I only mean that it would be a very interesting test of oneself.

If new experiences and contacts contribute to further self-development so that we have more to bring to life in ourselves, more to bring to life in others, then certainly they are good. They contribute to the prevention of boredom. If they don't so contribute, I am afraid they do not solve anything; they merely help us temporarily to kid ourselves.

II

HUSBAND — WIFE

by LAWRENCE S. KUBIE, M.D.[1]

It is only through what we call "clinical instruction" that one ever really learns the full import of human experience. But, unfortunately, I cannot utilize that combination of ward rounds, clinical seminars, and direct history-taking in this brief discussion of one fragment of the huge problem of the husband-wife relationship. We cannot follow that strange trailing parade of a group of doctors pausing in their rounds for a few moments at one bed, for half an hour at another. We cannot share with a young house physician the presentation of facts about a patient's life, the examination of the sick person, and the subsequent group discussion of what we have learned of one man's difficulties. Nor can we take histories ourselves and so, in direct interviews with a patient, gather the whole story of a human life.

I must instead describe to you an array of cases. In organizing them I have faced the dilemma that a few cases described in full might well seem to you special examples selected to argue some thesis; that, on the other hand, a multiplicity of examples sufficient to indicate the universality of marital problems will make it necessary to schematize and over-simplify

[1] Johns Hopkins. Clinical Professor of Psychiatry and Mental Hygiene, School of Medicine, Yale University.

II. Husband — Wife

each one. But we have to work within the limits of space at our disposal. I have not counted up my cases to see how many times they emphasize the man and his difficulties and how many times it is the woman and hers. My guess would be that it will come out about even; but if it does not, I can assure you that the shoe pinches each foot equally.

It is a difficult task to plunge into the middle of the most complex problem in human relationships, and this discussion is not designed to offer any easy solutions. It can hope at most only to illustrate a few of the individual problems that must be solved if we are ever to succeed in making of marriage the creative force that every sober student of the human comedy wants it to become. For there can be no question that divorce is always a tragedy, no matter how civilized the handling of it; always a confession of human failure, even when it is the sorry better of sorry alternatives. The psychiatrist studies divorce as the medical scientist goes to the autopsy table, there to learn from the ultimate consequences of human error its causes and how to avoid their repetition. Just as medicine has learned from illness and the autopsy most of what we know of normal physiology, so it is from marital failure that we must learn how to achieve marital success.

It would nevertheless be pleasant if I could begin on a brighter note than unhappiness and failure, offering you perhaps a neat little list of aphorisms, the do's and don't's of happy marriage. This might be excellent tactics, a device to win your sympathy before asking you to face up to tough and unpleasant realities. It would also be somewhat less than honest, however, since in the present stage of our knowledge no one has such easy answers to offer. We will profit by the experience of scientific medicine, and study marital illness before presuming to offer the intelligent reader any easy guides to marital health and happiness. Perhaps fifty years hence the answers can be given that all of us would like to have today.

Before going further, let me dispel one basic misconception. People think that the disruption of marriages is increasing. This is not true. In fact, quite on the contrary, it is decreasing. According to the most accurate available statistics,[2] from 1890 to 1940 there was a drop in the rate of disruptions from about 33 disruptions per 1,000 marriages to 30. In that same time, however, the cause of disruption has changed. In 1890, about 30 disruptions per 1,000 occurred because of death, and less than 3 per 1,000 by divorce. In 1940, marital disruptions by death had dropped from 30 to 21 per 1,000, whereas disruptions by divorce had risen from 3 to 9 per 1,000. This is a drop of 9 against an increase of 6. Thus the rising tide of divorces has not been large enough to offset the decrease in family disruption due to the decline in the death rate. *The surprising net result shows that more families are holding together in 1940 than in 1890.*

The difference remains, however, that divorce today is accomplishing some of the reshuffling of marriages which used to occur a few years ago through death. A friend of mine, of an old New England family in which there has never been a divorce, told me recently that both her great-grandfather and her great-grand-

[2] Paul H. Jacobson, Vital Statistics Analyst of the Metropolitan Life Insurance Company, in *American Sociological Review*, Vol. XV, No. 2, p. 235.

II. Husband — Wife

mother had married three times because of the early deaths of their respective spouses. Fifty years ago the death of one spouse was the rule during the age period between twenty and fifty. In other words, the divorce rate has increased largely because of the increased life expectancy in the middle years. Apparently the human race never has been mature enough for enduring marriages, a fact that was formerly obscured by early deaths, but that longevity has now exposed for study. Just as the statistics for cancer and heart disease have risen as we survive into the age period for these illnesses, so our divorce statistics are up because we live longer (Chart I, Jacobson). This increase in divorce in the middle years accounts for some increase in divorce in the early years of marriage, as an imitative phenomenon. It might be expected that young people who are brought up in an atmosphere in which divorce is accepted as a deplorable but not disreputable event would be more likely to turn to divorce quickly than young people who are brought up in a more rigid atmosphere. Available statistics are inadequate to establish this tendency precisely, but those that are available seem to indicate that divorce by unhappy example is not frequent enough to make a significant difference in the statistics.[3]

---

[3] Paul H. Jacobson, personal communication, April 1950: "A precise measure of the extent of 'impulsive divorces among young people' would require a case history study of a scientifically selected sample of marriages dissolved by divorce. From the curves shown in [Chart I], however, it does not appear likely that such divorces are an important component of the total picture. The trend of divorces has been upward, even among families of long standing. In fact, the curves at the

CHART I

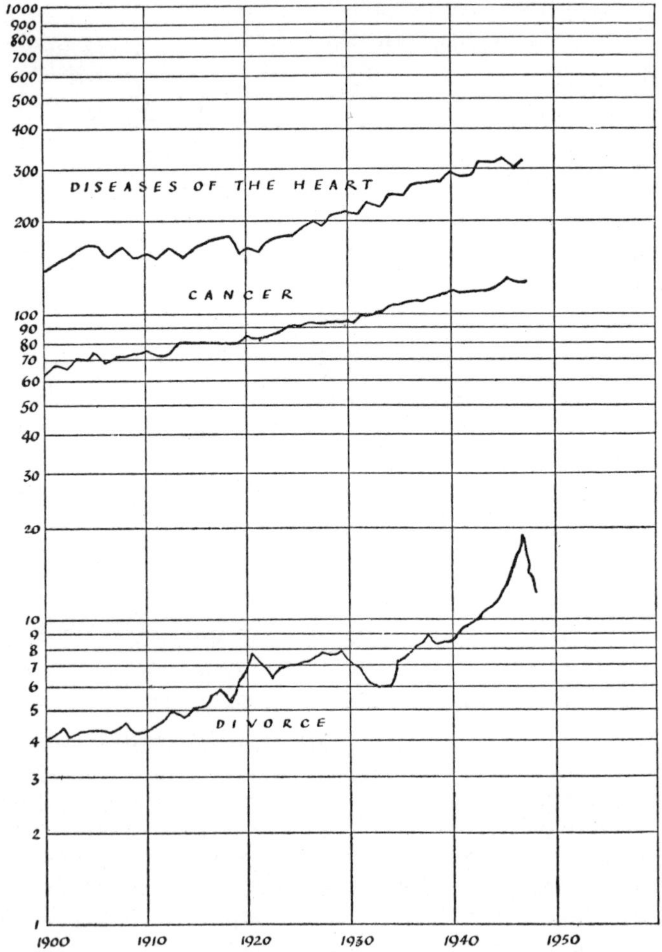

(CRUDE RATES UNADJUSTED FOR THE AGING OF THE POPULATION)
(Personal communication: Paul H. Jacobson, Vital Statistics Analyst,
Metropolitan Life Insurance Company; April 18, 1950)

II. Husband — Wife   [33

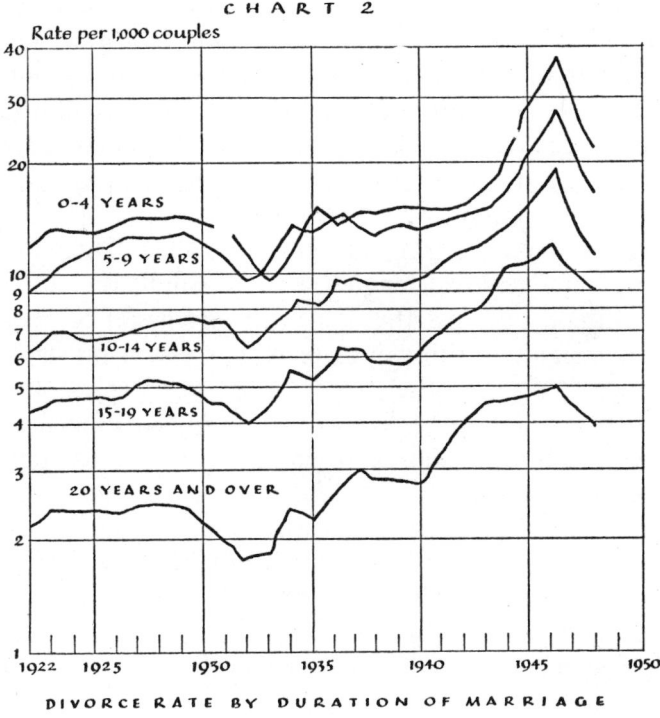

(From Paul H. Jacobson, in *American Sociological Review*, April 1950)

various durations of marriage are fairly parallel except during the late war and immediate postwar period, for those married less than 5 years. In other words, the sharp rise during the war resulted primarily from hasty war marriages, and also from the pushing ahead by several years of divorces which would have eventually occurred. In consequence, the recorded frequency of divorce was unduly high at the end of the war and in the first two postwar years, and this no doubt will be compensated for by rates below trend in 1948 through 1950 or 1951, after which the long-term upswing will again be apparent."

Let me digress for a moment to point out that, for adults at least, the psychological impact of a separation due to death may be quite different from the impact of a separation due to divorce. Small children may resent death as though it were a willful desertion; but for adults death leaves behind it no sense of willful abandonment, and therefore no personal humiliation, no personal sting, and no secret rage. There are only loneliness and longing. For the adult, therefore, separation and loss through death are easier to bear than separation through divorce. The effects on small children, on the other hand, are more complex, and much remains to be learned about the difference in the effects on children of losing a parent through death or through divorce. A detailed consideration of these questions is outside of the scope of this discussion; but I could not refer to the shift from the disruption by death to disruption through divorce without alluding to this example of the many psychological consequences of marital dissolution that remain to be explored.

Since, in spite of all of the social pressures that oppose it, divorce increases as the death rate falls, there is an implication that few of us are really mature enough for marriage, that in fact the human race is not really up to the complex and subtle task of being human. To be psychologically mature turns out to require a higher degree of special knowledge than most of us ever attain. The sources of marital discord are ubiquitous; they are to be found in each and every one of us.

Man has always had to struggle with his own dis-

II. Husband — Wife

content. Through the ages he has viewed this struggle moralistically; only in recent years has he come to see in it a scientific problem, a problem of health, a problem that can be solved only as we learn to co-ordinate the conscious and unconscious levels of psychological function in human life. Whenever man allows himself to moralize, he feels justified in blaming someone or something. Therefore throughout the long, dark, moralizing ages it has been man's way to blame something or someone outside himself for his discontent. He has blamed misfortune, he has blamed ill health, and above all he has blamed his marriages for it, when all the time its roots have been within himself. It is the influence on marriage of these universal sources of discontent that lie within all of us to which I want to call your attention.

This of course does not mean that there are no marriages that are intrinsically sick. Unfortunately there are many of these, many marriages that should never have been contracted, because they were made not in heaven but in that hell which we call the neurotic component of the so-called normal human being. I am not referring here to frivolous and irresponsible marriages, nor to marriages that are the product of a quick infatuation. I am talking of marriages made soberly and in good faith between thoughtful and sincere people, but under the predominant influence of unconscious psychological forces which compelled two individuals into an alliance that could not serve their unconscious needs. It will be my basic thesis that the major source of unhappiness between husband and wife is to be found in the discrepancies between their conscious and unconscious demands as these are expressed first in the choosing of a mate and then in the subsequent evolution of their relationship.

The best way to clarify this thesis will be through examples. Men and women are infinitely ingenious in their ability to find new ways of being unhappy together; so that even if I had unlimited space it would be impossible to illustrate every variety of marital misery. Therefore I will limit myself almost entirely to one aspect of the problem; namely, the difficulties that go into the choice of a mate. In some instances I shall have to consider troubles that arise later in the marriage, but my major emphasis will be on the unconscious forces that make it so difficult for people to know what they are seeking in marriage and on how this confusion influences the initial choice of a mate.

I look around me at the young people I know as they are scurrying into marriage. Most of them are reasonably happy and well-adjusted youngsters, friends of my own children, and children of friends, a few coming through the analytical office. As I watch the processes of selection, I feel as though I were watching a rigidly stylized dance, in which every act is transparently meaningful to the observer, but utterly meaningless to the blind dancer. Let me illustrate.

I think first of a young woman who had been left fatherless at an early age. Over a number of years it was evident to all of her friends, but not to herself, that she was driven by an obvious need to find in marriage a substitute father and an ally against her mother. She ran through a series of engagements with older men and finally married one who was within a year or so of her father's age, only to find in the end that a

II. Husband — Wife

substitute is never more than a substitute, and that in spite of the age discrepancy he wanted to be mothered as much as she wanted fathering. They ended in a snarl of bitter recriminations, each feeling cheated. I think of another young woman, whose entire existence has been dominated by a feeling that there was something secretly wrong with her. Consequently everything she ever did had concealment as one of its major secret purposes. She too was engaged many times to suitable young men, but always had to break the engagements to avoid the exposure of intimacy. Finally she was able to go through with a marriage to the suitor she cared least about, and then for only one reason: that it meant living in a distant and obscure land. She did not realize this, of course, until a last-minute change in his plans threw her into a turmoil of panicky indecision.

Needs that are obscure to the man or woman often take forms that are transparent to everyone else. One wholly unintellectual youngster married a college professor in an effort to triumph both over her own personal sense of degradation and over her mother. Another, the extremely intelligent and highly educated daughter of an intellectual professional woman, married a famous athlete of very little brain to make matter triumph over mind and mother. Another girl of extraordinary beauty, intelligence, and charm was compelled to choose an ill-favored, homely, poorly equipped, neurotic, and dependent man in an unconscious effort to hide herself. The discrepancy between the two shocked all of her friends; but just as the Rorschach or the Szondi tests may represent one's unconscious image of oneself, this unfortunate man represented this girl's unconscious distorted image of herself. In her choice of a husband she was saying to the world: "This is all that I am, and all that I am good for."

I might mention a strange yet frequent manifestation of the role of unconscious forces in the choice of a mate, those instances in which a youngster chooses someone who looks like himself, and those related instances in which the choice is of a diametrically opposite type. These are no accidents. They depend on the balance of unconscious self-love and self-hate in the structure of that personality. Recently I encountered a young couple who had worked out an excellent compromise, combining resemblance and contrast. They looked enough alike to have been twins. But one was very dark of hair and skin, the other equally fair.

Not long ago in a seminar at medical school we discussed a patient who illustrated another problem that frequently arises through the operation of unconscious psychological forces. Her mother was a vigorous, dominant, aggressive woman; the father was technically able but emotionally weak, insecure, and colorless. Before the house officer described it to me, I correctly predicted to the class in precise detail the kind of marriage I should expect that daughter to make. The young woman felt compelled to choose someone in her father's image, so that in her own marriage she could be as dominant a figure as her mother had been. Wholly unconsciously she had to duplicate in her own life everything she had hated most in her mother's behavior to her father. The ultimate outcome was equally predictable. She would hate the man if he submitted, as she had resented her father's weakness;

II. Husband — Wife

yet she would be forced automatically by the image of her mother in her heart to fight him violently if he opposed her. She ended in illness.

Let me turn to another group of examples. I think of two youngsters who had grown up insecure and lonely, seclusive and bookish in their tastes, in various ways apart from the general run of youngsters. They drew together through mutual sympathy and the compatibility of their intellectual and artistic interests, through their understanding of each other's needs and problems, and in some measure just because misery loves company. During their courtship they were all in all to each other. The sense of loneliness was gone. Each had an ally. Almost for the first time each had some place to go and someone with whom to share life. Each was literally all the world to the other.

Unfortunately, however, they married and soon discovered that when they faced the world together something quite unexpected happened to them. They could no longer be the whole world to each other. Instead they had to reach to the outer world to bring it into their joined lives. Yet each was still frightened of this world. In a sense each pushed the other, saying: "You go first." But neither could. So they began to get angry at each other. The separate and private misery that each had brought into the marriage and that originally had drawn them together was now compounded in a marriage that had been contracted in an unrealistic expectation that it would lessen that misery.

Instead, after marriage the unresolved neurosis of each was added to the neurosis of the other. That social shyness which had united them now became something hampering, which each resented in the other and ultimately drove them apart. They were learning bitterly and painfully a lesson that humanity as a whole has never learned: that no one has ever married himself out of a neurosis. Instead, when two young people are drawn into marriage by the lure of the other's illness, as happens so often, each will add the weight of his own neurotic infirmity to that of the other, with growing pain and resentment.

This confusion in the choice of a mate, and the unattainability of the unconscious purposes that determine this choice, may lead to unexpected and perhaps unpredictable changes after marriage. These may happen gradually or suddenly. An Englishman with active gregarious impulses had had a long and lonely battle with tuberculosis. During his recovery he met a girl with whom he shared many interests, among them a warm interest in human beings. Indeed, he was first drawn to her by the range and warmth of her friendships. After marriage an unforeseen change occurred. Neither of them had realized that it was possible for her to be sociable only as long as she was a bachelor girl, and that the moment she stepped into marriage her gregarious impulses would become so painfully inhibited that even with old friends she would become tense and awkward and silent. They had no way of foreseeing that she could be happy among other human beings only as a soloist, never as part of a duet. This was a streak of illness in her that could come to light only after marriage.

Without her ever having realized this, it was the reason that at the last moment she had several times shied away from marriage with highly compatible men.

II. Husband — Wife [41

It was only because her husband was still ill and therefore socially inactive that she had been able to marry him. None of this could they realize until after marriage; yet almost overnight she became as misanthropic as she had previously been warmhearted and outgoing, forcing her husband back into the loneliness and isolation in which his tuberculosis had imprisoned him for years. What this did to the rapport between them is easily imagined. They became bitterly unhappy and for a long time could not understand what had happened. She could never be induced to seek treatment, with the result that ultimately they broke up. It added greatly to his subsequent bitterness to discover that immediately after their separation she automatically became again the happy and gregarious person who had originally attracted him.

In another situation the shoe was on the other foot. Both were gregarious persons with innumerable friends. The man married a girl of beauty, wit, and intelligence who was in his own profession. He looked forward eagerly to taking her with him to meetings and to sharing with her the many activities in which he engaged. She came from a small and distant town, where she had made a name for herself, and she too looked forward to sharing their interests. But it did not work out that way. Instead he found himself making excuses to avoid taking her with him to meetings, or to avoid going at all. If he went with her he carefully avoided her, or became inexplicably sulky, silent, tense, and awkward. In this instance, fortunately, they had the wisdom to seek treatment before the relationship had become too strained for help. He found out why after marriage he had become unable to share any aspect of his life with a woman he loved and with whom he had shared everything during courtship. This automatic and paradoxical change was a manifestation of an unsuspected neurotic conflict, which through its various manifestations would have destroyed the marriage if it had been allowed to go untended.

Another unanticipated change in a relationship is often seen after the marriage of an aggressive woman who marries a man to dominate him without realizing what she is doing. I am not speaking of a comic-strip woman wrestler married to a Caspar Milquetoast, but of a much subtler version of the problem. I have in mind one such woman who in manner, clothes, build, and voice was gentle and tender. Yet, because of childhood hurts at the hands of her older brothers, she had a hidden but inflexible determination always to hold the upper hand in any relationship with any man. Unconsciously from adolescence on she had chosen men on that basis alone. When she finally married one of them, they soon found themselves in a dilemma. He was not weak, but he was a sweet and kindly man, always eager to do things to please her. After marriage they gradually became aware of a change. Without her realizing it, her victory had become empty; and she became restless. Unwittingly she was seeking new men to conquer. When he realized that she now not only took his submissiveness for granted but scorned it, he reversed his role and stood up to her. This was equally intolerable to her; and it was at this point, when the marriage was at the breaking-point, that the problem was brought to me.

An image keeps coming before my mind of some-

II. Husband — Wife

thing that happened nearly thirty years ago when I was at Johns Hopkins. We had a huge old cat and a tiny puppy. At night the cat would roll the puppy up and down the rug as though it were a ball of yarn. This continued even after the dog had grown much larger than the cat. It was amusing to watch the dog, now larger than the cat, tucking his head between his front paws and allowing himself to be rolled around. Then came an evening when in the most natural way the dog turned and began to roll the cat up and down the floor. The cat stood this reversal of roles for only a few minutes, then made one wild leap through an open window and was never seen again. More than once when there has been a reversal of roles in human marriages I have seen an outraged cat leap out that same window.

A variation on this theme occurred in the oldest of five sisters, a girl who throughout her childhood held a dominant position in the family because of her athletic skill, her beauty, and her great intelligence. Yet her successes gave her no sense of satisfaction, because they never enabled her to realize her unconscious goal. This was to be her father's only son and with him become the head of the family. This she had to carry out in her life by always choosing a man who in one way or another could be stamped as inferior. This dominated her courtship; but when the relationship was established as an engagement and finally as a marriage, the pain it caused her to be identified in public with an inferior man turned her love to hate, her admiration to scorn, and ultimately destroyed the relationship.

Another woman, who had been left motherless at

an early age, mothered her two younger brothers and her older brother as well. Indeed, she hid all the usual angry rivalry in this maternal quality. This made her lovable, but she became unable to treat any man as an equal. Throughout her life men could never be anything to her except children. This determined her choice of a husband, and also in part the subsequent deteriorating course of her marriage.

Interestingly enough, the same set of circumstances had a comparable effect on her older brother. It determined his choice of medicine and of gynecology as a career and made it impossible for him ever to love a woman who was not sick or in trouble.

There are many examples of the fatal discrepancy between conscious attainable demands and unconscious unattainable ones as a major source of marital discord. A widely prevalent type of problem is presented by the many men and women who marry with the one major unconscious purpose of finding a parent. This may take varied forms. The woman may unconsciously be marrying not her fiancé but his father or mother; or the man may be marrying his fiancée's mother or older sister or aunt, or, for that matter, her father. During the courtship, while the marriage is still in the offing, any vague feelings of discontent or of incompleteness can be balanced by the reassuring hope that a fuller contentment is just around the corner: when we get our own home, or when we have a child, or when we have ten children, or when we have a little more money, and so on. After marriage, however, the time comes when all such milestones will have been reached without dispelling feelings of emptiness and of unfulfillment. If we keep in mind the

II. Husband — Wife [45

unconscious and unattainable goal of the marriage, then the discontent is almost mathematically predictable. It has nothing to do with the potential compatibility of the couple's interests and standards.

As an example, I think of a woman who had been deeply hurt by her own father. He had rejected her completely, turning all of his affection to her brother. She married a man of whom she was deeply fond. On the surface this was because of his fine qualities; but unconsciously she chose him because she wanted his father to replace her own. Before her marriage the father-in-law-to-be had paid her a great deal of loving attention. She had not been married long, however, before she discovered that this had been only because of his passionate devotion to his son, her husband, whom indirectly he had courted by courting her affection. Thus the ultimate situation of her marriage duplicated with fantastic fidelity the situation of her childhood, with father-in-law and husband in the roles previously played by her own father and brother. In spite of her devotion to her husband, this rejection by her father-in-law stirred in her the old hatred of her brother, turned now in a blind fury against her husband. Had she not come for help, this would surely have destroyed her marriage.

Sometimes, because of a similarly unconscious need for a mother, the man may try to make a mother of his wife while at the same time the wife is trying to turn her husband into a father. Thus two immature people of middle age chose each other because of their very immaturity, two babes in the woods at forty. They married, to find out that each needed and wanted not a spouse but a parent. Although there is always a certain amount of maternal and paternal feeling in any relationship between a man and a woman, when this simultaneous and conflicting demand becomes the predominant goal of the marriage, each rejects the parental role into which the other is trying to force him, and each thereupon feels hurt and resentful. Then the marriage heads for trouble.

The unconscious need to reproduce something out of the past or to wipe out an old pain can influence marriage choices in many destructive ways. I think of two instances of young men who married their sisters' best friends, believing and feeling that they were in love with their young brides. They were indeed in love; not, however, with the girls they had married, but each with his own sister. I think of another young man who was deeply attached to his sister but also intensely hostile to her, for many reasons. Without knowing what he was doing, he fell in love with a girl and married her, not because of any essential compatibility between them, but solely because she was in every respect the opposite pole to his own sister. It was his way of getting back at the sister who had hurt him—hardly a sound basis for a happy marriage.

This need to wipe out an old pain or to pay off an old score comes up again and again. A young woman who had been the only girl and youngest in a large family grew up to be an overconscientious, thoughtful, responsible, and considerate youngster, but socially tense, awkward, and insecure. Her brothers, on the other hand, were charming, alcoholic wastrels who had made her childhood and adolescence miserable. What did she do? She fell in love with and married a man who was one of her brothers' best friends and

II. *Husband — Wife*

who shared all of their faults. She married him in an unconscious effort to wipe away the pain that these brothers had caused her through so many years. He on his part married her out of an unconscious homosexual attachment to her brothers. The pitiful outcome was of course predictable, because continuously over the years he put her through the same kind of hurt that had scarred her childhood.

Not long ago I saw a young man who had married himself into a predicament that was if anything even more painful. He had been an illegitimate child. Shortly after his birth his mother had married a man with whom she subsequently had a large family. My patient had been brought up as part of this family and was deeply devoted to his mother and to his stepfather. Like an automaton marching unconsciously to his doom, he tried to create in his own marriage a replica of his childhood by marrying his mother's image. That is, he married a girl who, like his mother, had had an illegitimate child by another man, seeking to find again in his marriage the warmth and affection of his infancy and childhood. Unfortunately for him, it did not work out that way: the girl proved to be a tramp. This was as though his own mother had betrayed him, and the hurt threw him into a deep depression.

There are men and women who show the domination of other types of unconscious purpose in their choice of a mate. I have seen men who repeatedly choose alcoholic or frigid or unfaithful wives; women who repeatedly choose brutal, alcoholic, impotent, or unfaithful husbands. In many of these women there is the history of an alcoholic father; and on analysis it becomes clear that the unconscious goal of the marriage was to cure the father's alcoholism in effigy, thus winning back the lost affection of the alcoholic father and at the same time proving that one can do a better job than one's mother, in that way triumphing over her.

Literature is full of tales of men who repeatedly choose women who will hurt them, women who cannot love a man. This is always in the service of unconscious needs. For instance, in their marriages human beings may try without knowing it to prove something about themselves that they themselves doubt obsessively. Thus men may try to prove that they can win love from an unloving mother or older sister, represented in the unloving wife they have chosen. Or they may have to prove their potency, or that they are not physically repulsive, by overcoming the grim aloofness of a woman who is essentially hostile to men. We do this consciously in other aspects of life, therefore it is inevitable that it should happen in marriage too. After all, if we have to prove that we are great mountain-climbers, we climb Mount Everest, not the Berkshires: and many men and women similarly have to prove the hard way that they are lovable.

The unhappiest feature of this need to prove something is its insatiability. Whenever the source of any self-doubt is unconscious, the need to prove it becomes endlessly repetitive. The simplest illustration of this is a hand-washing compulsion. The individual who suffers from such a compulsion knows that he does not have dirty hands. Nonetheless he has to play Lady Macbeth, crying: "Out, damned spot!" No

II. Husband — Wife

sooner does he finish scrubbing his hands than his secret doubts start welling up again, so that within a matter of hours, or even minutes, the compulsion to wash his hands again becomes overwhelming. The same thing occurs in the relationship between a man and a woman whenever a need to allay doubts whose roots are unconscious is the dominant force in the marriage. Under these circumstances the relationship becomes, after a while, incapable of satisfying the necessity to prove, irrespective of the essential quality of that relationship. Just as Joe Louis could not go on believing that he was the heavyweight champion of the world if he continued giving exhibition matches with the same stumble-bums, so a man with unconscious doubts about his potency cannot allay them by making love to the same woman all the time. Ultimately his neurotic need to prove himself will drive him into promiscuity. The same struggle with self-doubts has driven many a woman into the same path. Many a man with the reputation of being a Don Juan, many a woman who is known as a girl-around-town, is merely a poor unfortunate soul, running like mad, with the devil of self-doubt at his or her heels, finding a momentary surcease from torturing self-doubts through promiscuity. These self-doubts can be as unreal as a phobia of butterflies. The woman may be beautiful or the man a sexual athlete, and still they may be afflicted by fear. Thus on one occasion a young football star, a towering fellow with a magnificent build who had never in his life been impotent, came to me in tears because his home was about to break up. He was in love with his wife, but he was haunted by a fear of impotence which drove him against his will from woman to woman. This was merely an exaggerated example of something that in subtler form plays a role in many marriages.

It is hardly necessary to say that complicated forces that center on the problems of sexual adjustment can be important both in determining the choice of a mate and also in the subsequent evolution of a marriage. It *is* necessary, however, to make it clear from the start that an orgasm is not a panacea for all marital woe, and that sex can cause as much trouble when intercourse itself is physiologically successful as when it is unsuccessful. This may surprise you, but it is nonetheless true. I have never seen a marriage made or broken by sex alone, except in the case of frank perversions. I repeat that it is a gross oversimplification of this complex problem to think that the achievement of an orgasm marks the end of all difficulties. Paradoxically enough, it can sometimes be the start of trouble. There are individuals who bring into marriage such deep-seated feelings of sexual guilt that they can tolerate sex only as long as it is unsuccessful, and consequently react to an orgasm with guilt or panic. I have more than once treated a man who was on the verge of leaving his wife with whom he was physically happy, because each orgasm threw him into a panic and from panic into rage, and from rage into depression. I have dealt with women for whom an episode of happy and successful love-making always terminated in depression, followed by a subtle undercurrent of resentment that would express itself on entirely unrelated matters in the subsequent days. It was not for nothing that the ancient Latins coined the phrase: "*Post coitum triste.*"

II. Husband — Wife

Sometimes this leads the man to choose a frigid woman, or the woman to choose an impotent man. Each of these unhappy choices brings in its train its complicated frustrations. Thus the woman's frigidity —that is, her inability to have an orgasm—usually means to the man that there is something defective about him, something inadequate in him as a lover. This too can arouse anxiety, resentment, depression, and sometimes hypochondriacal fears of physiological inadequacy. Sometimes it drives the man to prove himself with other women, not realizing that he may have chosen his wife precisely because she was frigid and that he will run away from any woman who is sexually responsive, in spite of his need for the reassurance that such a woman could give him. These are complicated and unhappy dilemmas that grow out of our unconscious conflicts.

The woman who unwittingly always chooses impotent men similarly finds herself between Scylla and Charybdis. I think for instance of an extraordinarily beautiful woman whose secret image of herself was as homely, repulsive, and in some mysterious way inadequate. Her ideal male was a huge athletic hero, about whom she frequently dreamed. In real life, however, she turned only to diminutive men, beside whom she felt less inferior. She ran from one to another in a vain attempt to find reassurance. Another woman in a similar situation married an impotent man and then was tormented by the feeling that his impotence was her fault, which proved and confirmed to her her horror of her own body. For a time this drove her into a life of promiscuity, which she abhorred and which in turn made her deeply depressed. Each single erotic episode gave her the same momentary relief from unbearable pain that a man with a hand-washing compulsion gets from washing his hands. I would emphasize, however, that in both cases the relief is only momentary. Within a few minutes the torturing self-doubts start up again.

Paralleling the woman who lived her fantasy-life with huge athletes and her real life with little scholars, there is the man who because of his own unconscious feelings of genital inferiority has to choose a small woman, or a woman with a small mouth and small breasts, with a dim notion that there will not then be such a discrepancy in size between them. Then, however, he feels publicly humiliated, as though he had proclaimed to the world his genital inadequacy.

There is also the perplexing yet familiar phenomenon of the man who loses his potency with any woman whom he loves and respects, but who can be potent with one whom he scorns. I have even known a man who had had a happy affair with a woman for many years during which his wife was hopelessly ill. He married this mistress eagerly after his wife's death, only to become impotent with her on their wedding night and ever after. Comparable reactions occur in women as well—in anyone, in fact, in whom the taboo on sex is so deep-seated that it can be shared only in the gutter.

These distortions occur subtly or grossly and in varying degrees of severity with great frequency. They are not rare oddities. Their frequency is due to the fact that we grow up with a profoundly distorted attitude toward the human body. It is indeed a remark-

II. Husband — Wife

able fact that we have been human beings for quite a number of years and that we still do not accept the anatomical differences between the body of a man and the body of a woman. It is not accepted in art. Anyone who goes to the galleries can see that a part of the artistic drive is a subtle effort to disguise and distort and alter the reality of the body, either by minimizing these differences or else by burlesquing them. We find the same thing in fashions both for men and for women through the ages. We find the same thing in bed. It is not for nothing that Anatole France in *Penguin Island* pointed out that when the penguins turned into human beings they lost their virtue only when they put on clothes—that is, only when they hid the rejected realities of the body. Man is like that; and no young man or young woman comes to marriage without bringing along some measure of this deep-seated problem to overcome. Marriage demands that he overcome his secret rejection of his own body, and of the body of his partner. This he often cannot do. Not infrequently a compromise forms in his mind as an unconscious fantasy of finding some mysterious middle sex, some sex that is neither male nor female, or else both in one. We find this in the effeminization of men's fashions and in the masculinization of women's.

The inability to accept ourselves as we are influences the choice of the marriage partner in a quite characteristic way, frequently forcing the young man or woman to choose someone who resembles himself or herself, as though each were marrying his own alter ego of the opposite sex. Here again an unconscious impulse can never be realized in actuality; and the symbolic act of marrying your own counterpart of the opposite sex leads inevitably to bitter and seemingly inexplicable disillusion. The same confused rejection of the body also expresses itself in those labored variations on techniques of intercourse which fill the pages of stupid books on the sexual aspects of marriage.

In all of these problems it is much easier to place the blame on the partner than to say that there is some subtle discrepancy between what I think I want and what I actually want in the unconscious depths of me.

Most perplexing of all is the fact that a marriage that starts under completely happy auspices can sometimes go to pieces because of that very happiness. These are situations in which a man or woman has been so hostile to a parent that he or she cannot tolerate resembling the parent. This can even occur when the parent's marriage has been so happy that the child rightly or wrongly has felt excluded from it. As a consequence even a happy marriage can be intolerable to that child, because it forces on him an identification with a hated parent. This starts a deep surge of tension, rebellion, and self-hatred. The hate that had originally been for the parent now becomes a self-hate; and the result is a paradoxical depression as a reaction to a happy marriage, with ultimate rejection of the marriage itself. These are complex and tragic paradoxes, yet we cannot pretend to ourselves that the problem is any simpler than this.

There are also all the choices made out of insecurity —the man who is too anxiety-ridden to stand on his own feet and who marries for external security of one

II. *Husband — Wife* [55

kind or another; the woman who must have a prominent and successful husband, but not a busy one (that is, the woman who wants to be married to the President of the United States but only on vacation).

Finally there are the competitive unions: the man who chooses beauty but cannot tolerate his wife's attractiveness and popularity; the woman who chooses success but cannot tolerate her husband's career, or even his physical prowess. For instance, one woman who was an intensely jealous rival, but who could never let herself express any of this rivalry in open competition, married her gladiator. That is, she married a highly successful, highly competitive businessman-athlete, and then could never share in or enjoy any of his triumphs, but belittled his victories and compulsively made fun of him whenever his dexterity failed him.

Thus the difficulties of maintaining a happy relationship may start the moment that the period of courtship is over—indeed, the moment that uncertain pursuit has turned into victory. The fact that two people who have been completely happy during a thoughtful and serious courtship can become equally unhappy once this relationship is established in marriage is one of the most frequent, often overlooked, and at the same time most difficult problems that marriage faces. It is as universal as a common cold, and just as tough an adversary.

I hope that I have made it clear that the choosing of a mate is one of the most confused steps that a human being takes in life; and this not primarily because he chooses a mate whose interests and habits are incompatible with his own, but because each of the pair is ignorant of the unconscious purposes that determine their respective choices. This is why hasty and impulsive unions may stand up as well as those which have been made with the greatest possible conscious foresight. Both can miscarry whenever the unconscious goals that exercise a preponderant influence are left out of account.

Certainly, as our examples have shown, there are many marriages, made slowly and on the basis of compatible conscious interests and harmonious conscious goals, which should have been sound, but which, as the unconscious goals diverged, went on the rocks. Those very activities which before marriage had been shared happily can unexpectedly become after marriage the source of bitter unhappiness. So subtle are these changes, indeed, that the quality of the courtship may be no index of what the marriage will be. This is a tragic and serious problem. To my way of thinking it is perhaps one of the most important challenges that face us.

Furthermore, it is obvious that the state of being in love is no guide. It is an obsessional state, which like all obsessions often is driven by unconscious anger. The transition from that strangely ambivalent obsession which we call "being in love" to the capacity really to love another human being is one of the most important and difficult and intricate phenomena of human life, yet it is only in recent years that it has been subjected to critical scientific study.

All of this brings me to the conclusion that one of the most fundamental challenges that confront us today is to discover how human beings, young and old,

II. Husband — Wife

can be taught to distinguish between their conscious and attainable goals and needs on the one hand, and their unconscious and unattainable goals on the other. Until we can do this, the problem of human happiness, whether in marriage or out, will remain unsolved.

This is a large order. Perhaps the answer will come through a basic and fundamental change in our entire system of education, a change which recognizes that no matter how well a human being is educated in chemistry, physics, economics, history, or literature, he remains a barbarian unless he knows something about himself. Self-knowledge in depth, which has been the forgotten factor of our educational system, must become instead its primary focus. Since Socrates, the ideal of knowing ourselves has not been new. Psychiatry has only added a deeper understanding of what knowing oneself implies. Like good intentions, self-knowledge is of little value unless it penetrates to the unconscious levels of the human spirit. On this depends the future of marriage.

There is a group of questions that in different forms ask the same thing:

1. Since human beings are imperfect, since few of us have insight into our unconscious purposes when we make our marriage choices, since few of us are emotionally mature when we marry, and since there often are unanticipated changes between the choosing period and the living period, how can we be sure of making a

right choice? How can we guide young people or advise them? Are there any ways of testing or any indexes?

My answer to these questions must be that in the present stage of our knowledge we have no sure guides. Here our position is comparable to that of medicine in relation to many illnesses. We can diagnose the existence of an illness, and even know something of its nature, long before we are able either to prevent it or to cure it. The same thing is true of these problems of marriage choice. We have no indication that a battery of psychological tests would help us here. Furthermore, apart from the fact that it would be impossible practically, we do not even know that universal analysis in the adolescent years would necessarily make for happier marriages. We can only say that if we strive to modify our whole educational process so as to give every human being a deeper insight into himself and his own needs from an early age; if self-knowledge in depth is no longer the forgotten factor of our whole educational system; if as a result of this we achieve earlier emotional maturity to keep pace with our intellectual and physical maturity; then conscious and unconscious goals are likely to come much closer together in marriage choice. When we achieve this as part of many basic cultural changes and developments, then I think we can look forward to sounder choosing and therefore to sounder marrying.

In other words, what I am saying is that the capacity to choose wisely and soundly and therefore to live in harmony depends upon developmental processes that must start in the early years, because they affect the rate of maturation of the personality as a whole

II. *Husband — Wife*

and the ultimate harmony between conscious and unconscious components in that personality. This is of far more importance in marriage than is any kind of marriage counseling. The need for marriage counseling is in itself by implication a confession of our cultural failure.

I would also point out that by implication some re-examination of the romantic tradition is indicated; and a careful and objective study of the obsessional quality of infatuation must be made. Most studies of obsession are, of course, quite unpleasant. Infatuations happen to be, in balance, pleasant obsessions, at least while they last. But an obsession is an obsession; and whether pleasant or unpleasant, it is never healthy nor conducive to ultimate happiness.

Another group of questions focuses on an important practical issue:

2. Granting that most marriage choices are made in the dark as compromises between obscure conscious and unconscious purposes that are in conflict, what then can one do about this? Does partial insight or any degree of retrospective insight help?

The answer is that of course insight may help, in one of two ways: It may and occasionally does show that the marriage should never have been made. When this happens, two human beings instead of tearing each other to pieces, agree in all friendliness that each made an innocent error of judgment in good faith, and the tie can be dissolved with a minimal amount of injury or pain. In many other situations, however, a recognition of the unconscious as well as the conscious goals makes it possible for the married couple to help each other work out a harmonious compromise between their various purposes. Many a marriage has not only been saved, but actually been made deeply significant and constructive and harmonious through insight of this kind.

Another group of questions raises a pertinent problem:

3. Has the marriage that is prearranged by parents, and in which the two young people take no part in the choosing, any advantages over our system?

Frankly, I do not believe that it has either advantages or disadvantages. I do not believe that the unconscious purposes of two sets of scheming parents are likely to serve our aspirations much better than the unconscious purposes of a pair of immature youngsters. No, I am sure there is no solution as simple as that. Nor do we have any evidence that any one race or national group has come closer to solving this problem than any other.

Another group of questions focuses on the question:

4. Would trial marriages solve the problem?

I have to say that I cannot answer this. On theoretical grounds I doubt that trial marriages would be a solution. But since they have never been given widespread trial in an atmosphere that welcomes them, but have always had to be made surreptitiously,

II. *Husband — Wife* [61

I cannot say. We know that some people can learn from experience, and others never are able to do this. This is true in every other aspect of life, and it is certainly true in marriage. We know people who, because of the shape and pattern of their unconscious problems, make the same mistakes in their choices over and over again. This can happen in a trial marriage just as well as in a real marriage. I should not expect trial marriages to hold any magic in meeting this problem.

Finally, the question is asked:

5. **How does it happen that some people manage to make happy marriages?**

This is a searching question; and it is related directly to an equivalent issue: namely, how does it happen that some people manage to live not only without symptomatic neuroses but without even the burden of masked neurotic disturbances of the so-called normal. We cannot answer this. We do not yet know enough. In medicine it is always true that we first begin to understand the normal by the study of illness. Thus the study of pathology throws light on normal physiology; and the study of neurotic deviations from normality is slowly building up an understanding of psychological normality. But we are not yet able to say *why* some few people develop normally whereas most of us develop neurotic episodes in early childhood which leave neurotic scars throughout our lives. In the present stage of our knowledge of human development those who escape this experience are happy accidents. They hold up to us a shining hope. For if this can happen to a few people, we should be able to learn how to make it possible for most. When we have the answer to that problem, we shall know the answer to the problem of why, in spite of their lack of any deep personal insight, by accident some people have been able to make happy marriages. And when we have that knowledge, a happy marriage will no longer be a happy accident. This, however, is going to take long and hard and serious study on the part of the human race. It will not be solved by clinging to formulas of the past which have not worked.

I think, as I have said before, that we may best approach this outcome through: (1) a modification of the romantic tradition, so we may cease to look upon an obsessional state as the highest artistic, æsthetic, and spiritual experience of life; (2) a fundamental change in the processes of education, so that individuals grow up without the cleavage that exists at present between the conscious and unconscious aspects of the personality; and (3) the development of techniques by which such cleavages as do occur can be rapidly knit together, so as to maintain the integrity and unity of the personality as a whole, especially as the young person approaches marriage.

You will see that I have no easy answers. I take the position that marital stress is nothing new in life; that it has been obscured by early deaths, that it is one of the oldest and one of the most important problems in human culture because of its influence on children as well as on grownups, and that it can be solved only by a frank facing of the fact that the capacity of one human being to love another human being is the highest and most important challenge with which the human

II. Husband — Wife

spirit is confronted, and that every effort of modern science must be brought to bear upon it.

As I have said before, we have discovered that it is a difficult and complex thing to be a human being and that the human race has not yet grown up to it. Let me add that part of the capacity to be a human being is the capacity of one human being to love another. This is a peculiarly human challenge. Let us not pretend that it is an easy one to be solved by any ancient formulas. On the other hand, let us not turn our back on it just because it is difficult.

III

PARENT — CHILD

by FREDERICK H. ALLEN, M.D.[1]

I WANT to move away from the two extremes that frequently dominate the discussion of parental, particularly maternal, responsibility. One extreme stresses the sentimental view of the beauties of motherhood; the other stresses the dangers and perversities of this role. The latter has been the more dominant in recent years, both in discussion and in the considerable literature on this subject. The first emphasis minimizes the fact that this relationship arouses a variety of emotional reactions in both parent and child which are human and natural; the second emphasis, stressing as it does the dangerous and destructive potential in the parental relation to a child, tends to create a belief that parents are bad for children. Neither emphasis helps us to understand the vital quality in these roles and the creative power inherent in the family when they are appropriately developed.

A psychiatrist is usually expected to stress the destructive influences of the parent on a child, since his professional responsibilities bring him into a close contact with their difficulties. The fact that he sees so much of the difficult side must be balanced with the

[1] Johns Hopkins. Clinical Professor of Psychiatry, Medical School, University of Pennsylvania; director of the Philadelphia Child Guidance Clinic.

III. Parent — Child

equally significant fact that he also knows, from clinical experience, how much parents and children can do in restoring the values of their separate but related roles when they regain a feeling of self-respect. Neither parent nor child is helped by any approach that seeks to confront them with their mistakes and to make them aware of how bad they have been.

Precisely because parental relationships have such a creative influence on the healthy growth of a child, they will also bring about many opportunities for friction and conflict. Many of these conflicts are resolved out of the day-to-day living of parents and children. Many, however, are more serious; and the problems that develop in our children grow out of unhealthy elements that gain ascendancy in a family in which a parent and a child are trying to find a way of living together. For this reason it is important to acquire more and more understanding of family dynamics, and to make this information generally available to help parents and children fulfill the healthy potential inherent in their roles.

Instead of focusing, therefore, on case material, which after all emphasizes individual lack of understanding and mismanagement of the parent-child relationship, I wish to take a positive approach to some of the dynamic elements in this relationship.

The family has existed in one form or another through the whole history of the human race. It is the basic unit in any culture. In the family the drama of growth unfolds. Its setting provides a framework within which the child first experiences his aliveness and awakens to the reality that he is a separate individual. But this first awakening brings him into a new relatedness to the mother, who was the biological hostess through the period of his intra-uterine development. Now as he starts his separate life process she has a different but equally important function to fulfill because he cannot live without all she must give. His awakening, therefore, has a dual quality: he awakens as an individual, while feeling his dependence upon another individual external to himself. Two sets of forces now go into action. First, he is a separate living unit capable of sustaining life by means of the biological equipment with which he starts. Gradually new uses can be made of his capacities, and from their uses emerges an individual, separate and different from those who gave him his equipment. He will need to maintain this individuality throughout the whole journey of growth.

But the development of these individual forces is modified because each child is born into a world of other individuals who, through the accumulation of their experience and customs, have a fairly well-defined idea of the kind of individual he should be. Social or external forces go into action to help the child become an individual in a world of relationship to others. He must become a member of a group while at the same time he must preserve himself as an individual.

In the interaction between these two forces, the biological and the social, there emerges the dynamic quality of the family. The adult and the child—one the giver, the other the receiver—begin to find through living experience how these forces can operate in harmony. They can never operate separately, but are always separate. The biological forces constantly op-

III. Parent — Child

erate to maintain the integrity of the individual; the social forces operate to preserve the continuity of the culture and to maintain the integrity of the group.

At first these forces seem to operate against each other. On the one hand, the child is attempting to preserve his individuality, while on the other hand he meets other forces that seem to be preventing this achievement. In healthy individual development within the normal family setting we find these two forces coming into relative harmony with each other. I purposely say "relative" because there is always an element of conflict.

In our psychiatric jargon we tend to think of conflict as the evidence of trouble. Frequently it is; but when we examine how the social and biological forces act together, how a child finds that he can use the standards of society and what the parent has to give, we begin to realize that some conflict is always present between parent and child, between young and old, or between parent and parent. The very fact of difference creates some conflict, which can be one of the important motivations for growth. Conflict, therefore, can be regarded as of the essence of all that is healthy in life. Each human being's problem is to learn how to utilize the motivations that are stirred by this conflict. We know how this principle operates in mechanics. A train would not be able to move along its tracks without the element of friction; but sometimes we overlook that principle in our living together. In our efforts to smooth the way so as to rid living of conflict, we may take out of life one of its most potent developmental forces.

Within the setting of the family the child has first

experiences and contacts with a world in which he is going to live and become an individual. He gains his first awareness of being a separate person. Here adults begin to function as parents and to fulfill the responsibility of directing his growing up. They make it possible for him to live in a setting in which he awakens to a realization that he is not just whatever the parents want him to be. He is a new creative force capable of becoming, within the limits of his biological equipment, an independent, socially responsible individual.

In the framework of the family the roles of mother and father are defined and fulfilled, and I want to examine some of the essential features of these adult roles. A man and a woman who have found values in their roles as husband and wife now find new and different opportunities in the roles of father and mother. Each role should nourish the other. The father role and the mother role are achieved through maturity. Those parents who feel: "Now I am going to live for my child," narrow their lives around that formula. Starvation of the adult interests of parents creates real obstacles in achieving healthy parental roles and thus obstructs the child's discovery of the value of being a child.

Let us look first at the unique qualities of the mother role. The accumulated experience of every culture defines in a broad way the function of the mother. Customs, traditions, and knowledge provide each new mother with a supporting framework to help her. She will borrow from the experience of other mothers, following some of the prescribed rules current in the particular culture in which she lives and rejecting others. But she will experience her own in-

III. Parent — Child

dividual feelings in her role as mother, which becomes unique and vital because she is living it. She will discover there are no fixed and final rules and no textbook pattern that will supply all the answers to her many questions or will allay her natural doubts and anxieties. She learns that being a mother is quite different from what she anticipated. The significant answers are found in her own day-to-day experience, reinforced by the knowledge available in her own culture.

During the life of the child before birth, the mother's life is more important than its own. Many factors make this true. She is the hostess to a new individual that grows in her and feels like an integral part of herself. Her biological and emotional investment in this new life is large. It requires many adaptations and arouses many emotional reactions. The thrill of creativeness is tempered by anxiety and concern for her own safety. Hope and fear, joy and irritation, desire for a child and resentment against what is required of her to have one—these are the natural and human feelings experienced by a woman in the process of fulfilling the biological purpose of becoming a mother.

The birth experience ushers in a new and equally important period of adaptation. The child is now a separate living entity. The shift from being the biological hostess to being the guardian of a new life brings new responsibilities and new emotional reactions. The child cannot live without her care. She nourishes a living organism that is no longer an undifferentiated part of herself. She now has the opportunity and responsibility of directing the slowly emerging capacities inherent in the child and helping him to become an individual, separate and different from her. The close bond between mother and child begins to change as the child begins to feel his separateness.

From the infant's point of view, if it is permissible to assume he has one, the mother exists as though she were still a part of him. In the early days of his living, there is little in his experience that enables him to have any sense of being a person apart from her. When he is hungry, she satisfies him. When he cries, she comes to him. He learns early that his discomforts and the relief from them are associated with the mother's presence and what she does with and to him. The infant reacts promptly and impulsively to those stimuli arising from any feeling of discomfort, such as a hunger pang. He makes this known by a cry, but the mother responds to this according to a plan. The child asserts his need, and the mother, in responding, introduces a directing influence in the child's life. When she follows a plan of feeding the child at stated intervals, she is doing more than satisfying a child's need for food. She is also meeting his need for direction, and thus helping him to take his first step away from action-in-response-to-an-impulse toward action-based-on-some-direction-of-impulse. Eventually this leads to a control that the child begins to exercise himself.

True, the mother imposes her own will on the child. Feeding schedules are arranged so as to meet the needs of the child, but also are designed to consider the convenience of the mother. Both are important for a healthy relation. The mother who says of herself: "My feelings don't count, I am only concerned about what is good for my child," is starting off on a false basis. When she annihilates herself to that extent, she can-

III. *Parent — Child*

not provide any of the experience of outside reality which a child needs from her. Trying to annihilate herself means that the mother can never allow a child any discomfort, since that would be proof that she is not supplying all the child's needs. I have known mothers who feel it important to anticipate all a child's needs. This denies a child one very important need: the need to be aware of having a need. The mother who knows the importance of this can help the child to begin to reach out and satisfy some needs through what he does rather than through what others do for him.

The mother who, in fulfilling her role in a natural way, both gives and withholds, brings the growing child into a friendly relation to a world that is planned not just for him but that has a real place for him which he must have a real part in finding. It is true that the child has to do more adapting to the world he lives in than that world to him. Whether we like it or not, this is the kind of a world in which a child will become an adult, since every child is born into an organized world and to parents who prior to his arrival have found a way of living that holds some satisfaction for them. This may seem like a harsh statement, but the harshness is tempered and even removed by the knowledge that the parents, particularly the mother, can allow the child more and more opportunity to expand his little world and to use his own developing capacities. No mother with a common-sense regard for the child and for herself will risk exposing a child to a danger from which he can be protected. But, on the other hand, she will not exaggerate her responsibility to the point of seeking to shield the child from those pains and anxieties which naturally belong to the life of a growing child.

In the normal fulfillment of the mother role the mother respects both her role and the child. The child then, in using and responding to her affection and direction, begins to feel a sense of dignity for himself as a child. Such a mother gives without binding the child to her, and helps him move out toward other relations, the most important of which is the relation of the child to the father.

The father fulfills his place in the new family drama in a way quite different from the mother's. He may present himself to his friends as the proud possessor of a child and receive their congratulations and hand out the cigars; but after a few days he resumes his daily routine. In the main his own life goes along about as usual except that his wife is less free to do with him the things they have enjoyed together before this new responsibility was undertaken.

For the infant the mother is the focus of his awakening interest in the world about him. The father, who is not present as much, is for the infant another person. His entry into the child's orbit is gradual and becomes more meaningful as the child moves out of the closeness to the mother which infancy requires. The more the child develops a sense of himself as a person, the better able he becomes to include other people within his widening orbit.

The difference in the child's relation to the mother and to the father can be described in this way: The relation to the mother exists as very close from birth and changes and becomes less close and less that of a dependent as he grows. The relation to the father does

III. Parent — Child

not exist at birth, but is formed from the waking up of the child through his own living experience. In the normal family created by the maturity of the adults, these differences in the mother and father roles are not the source of tension. The fact that the mother has a different and more important role to fulfill will not threaten a mature man who has found value in what he is and what he has to do. The mature mother can give all she has to a child without the need of perpetuating the child's dependent state. She will give with the central goal of helping the child to acquire the capacity to meet his own needs and to have other relationships.

But we can readily see how complications can enter this family drama when the father feels threatened by the difference in roles. Too frequently we see a father having to exaggerate his importance to make up for feeling unimportant. We see a father who develops a feeling of being neglected reacting with hostile attitudes toward the child with whom he now shares the mother. In some instances the father will have little to do with a child and becomes unduly irritated by the inconveniences that inevitably occur because of a child's presence in a household where before there were only adults.

The mother may contribute to this type of tension by giving up too much of her adult life for the child and becoming unduly responsible. Such a mother tends to keep the child to herself and leaves little place for the father. In a healthy family life, adult interests and activities are modified by the arrival of a child, but they are not eliminated.

The important element in family unity is that these

different roles function freely and with understanding of the values growing from their difference. Upset one and the family balance is thrown off. The father who withdraws or who tries to take the role of the mother not only upsets his own place; he also disturbs the natural operation of the mother role. The result is the disturbance of the child. Conversely, he best finds the value of being a child when he is provided with the natural support and direction of both the father and the mother.

Normally the father will see and feel something of himself in his son. In varying degrees he lives again in his son. There is both value and danger in this, but in stressing the danger there has been a tendency to overlook the normal and healthy aspects of this feeling of a father for his son. It is true that the boy child will first see the father as a threat to his more complete relation to the mother, which he begins to relinquish as he grows up. No child will let this relation change without some struggle and without help. But the father who takes his place in the family naturally and responds to the developing interest of the child in him will be the one who provides the child, whether boy or girl, with the bridge he needs as he moves away from dependence on his mother. The father who can see something of himself in his boy can provide the boy with his first pattern of what he wants to be himself. The boy needs this and can make healthy use of pride in his father while gaining more confidence in himself. With this confidence he can begin to assert his own difference from his father.

The mature father who does not need to re-create

III. *Parent — Child* [75

himself in his son will find his satisfaction in the boy's growing capacity for independent action. He can provide the boy with a masculine ideal by simply being himself. This can mean that he will fulfill his responsibility as father by taking a hand in the boy's development. He can exercise an important influence in helping the boy to shape his interests and to develop codes for behavior, without trying to re-create himself and live again in the boy. Some fathers fall into the false idea, sometimes called "modern," that the only way to make friends with their sons is to get down to their level, to do all the things they do and be interested in all that is a part of a boy's life. Here the false part again concerns the important element of difference. In feeling the need to get down to a boy's level, the father is trying to erase his own adultness on the assumption that his "bigness" presents a barrier to companionship. The result is confusing to both adult and child. A boy may rather play ball with another boy of his own age than with the zealous father who feels he must play regardless of his own interest and ability.

The best companionship between father and son develops as they come to know each other as father and son—not as two boys together, but as adult and child. As such the father can develop an active interest in his boy's activity, and the boy can feel an interest in what the father is and does. Spontaneously a father can play with his boy and the boy with him because there is pleasure and not merely duty in it. Just as naturally a father can go about his own activity without feeling guilty of depriving his son of his presence. Real companionship is not measured by a time schedule, but rather by the feeling of interest and respect each comes to have for the other as they live together.

Books have been written stressing the fact that babies and children are human beings. But equal stress can be laid on the fact that parents are human beings. They have feelings and sometimes can feel irritation and anger over things children do. Patience has been elevated to the status of a virtue. This quality can cease to be a virtue when it is achieved by suppressing natural feelings. An unhealthy situation occurs when a parent feels the need of always maintaining an attitude of calm and reasonableness. Parents should try to train the child to live with flesh-and-blood human beings, not with plaster statues.

Children test out a parent in their efforts to grow on their own terms. They can be very demanding and unreasonable, and need to feel the impact of a parent's firmness. They do so when the parent gives vent to his own feelings. A good example of this was given by a parent who described her reasonable efforts to get her seven-year-old son to go to bed. He had as many reasons for not going as the mother had for it. After a half hour of this she became angry and said: "You go to bed, and go because I say so." The boy replied: "Well, why didn't you say so in the first place?" and peacefully went to bed. Only when parental feelings of irritation or anger become dominant and supplant the gentler feelings do we encounter problems. The child needs and expects to receive adult direction and control.

In this connection a few comments on discipline may be helpful. It is a curious phenomenon that when-

III. Parent — Child

ever we speak of discipline most people immediately think of punishment. The two words seem to be synonymous, yet when we analyze the origin of the word *discipline*, we find it has the same root as *disciple*. *Discipline* is a positive word and conveys the responsibility of leadership, of defining for a child a life that holds reality and purpose. Discipline as a positive form is as important in the life of a child as food and shelter. A healthy concept of discipline should grow out of the respect that the parents have for their own adult strength, and at the same time should include a basic respect for the individuality of the child.

While discipline is not synonymous with punishment, that element is present in any adult-child relation. When punishment becomes the dominant purpose of discipline, it means that obedience is expected to be absolute and automatic. Such a concept accentuates negative behavior in both parent and child, and serious conflicts occur.

There are many inevitable dilemmas that emerge as parents fulfill their responsibilities. It is natural and right that parents bring into their directive efforts the attitudes and desires and expectations that have been important in their own lives. Naturally they want a child to develop qualities they can like. These are qualities they have found valuable in themselves. They also want to prevent the emergence in their child of qualities they don't like either in themselves or in others. They bring to bear on their children the accumulation of their own experience, acquired in their own growing up. This may seem like imposing a personality pattern on a child. To some extent it is, and in some degree this is inevitable and necessary.

Yet the goal of parental efforts is the development of a new individual, not of a rubber-stamp imitation of themselves. So the dilemma all parents face is this: how can they direct and guide a child of their creation, and give it all that is essential and desirable, and yet encourage the development of those differences which make for a mentally healthy and creative individual? How can they encourage creativeness in the object of their creation? How can they discipline and direct and teach and do all that falls within the parental responsibility and still encourage the independence of thought and action which characterizes a healthy boy or girl?

Satisfactory answers to this dilemma can be seen in many normal, healthy families who may never have heard of psychiatry or never have read a book on how to bring up children. The outstanding qualities in such families are spontaneity and naturalness, which grow out of both self-respect and sensitive respect for the other person. Such healthy give-and-take leads to a readiness both to assume and to allow responsibility. Healthy parents can be wrong. They can show irritation when that human reaction is appropriate. Their children can do their rebelling along with their conforming without disturbing the dignity and authority of the parent. In such an atmosphere the dilemma of growth is solved through the natural experiences of mature people; there is individuality for each, but there is also a sense of group responsibility.

It is important for parents to realize that the child in growing also has a dilemma to solve. He is born into a world to which he has to adapt rather than have the world adapted to him. He is the product of

III. Parent — Child

forces that operate outside of himself. He didn't have anything to say about being born or about who were to be his parents. He finds himself in a world of established customs, traditions, and expectations. From the first moment he starts to breathe and to cry out, forces from without impinge upon him to mold him in the pattern of the culture of which he becomes a part. He has the problem of finding out through living how he can be an individual in a world that, from his point of view, seeks to take his individuality away. As he grows and becomes a better-defined personality, he reacts more and more against the limits and expectations that define the boundaries of his living. He senses the interest and desire of the parent to mold him. Call this training, habit formation, discipline, or what you will, the child is aware of the efforts of his parents, and later of his teachers and others, to change him and make him into the kind of person they can like.

In stating the dilemma for the child I am not referring to exaggerated, tense, and anxiety-charged efforts of a parent to shape a child's personality. These efforts exaggerate the growth dilemma, but they do not create it. I am referring to the normal functioning of the parent role in every family, and am recognizing that an adult cannot be a parent without exercising a strong influence on the direction of the child's growth.

So for the average child his dilemma emerges out of his growing up and arises when he senses his own difference. It is a natural and healthy thing for a child to want to be liked and to have the approval of those who love him. But as he grows, he becomes puzzled how he can be what his mother and father want him to be and at the same time be himself and not simply a product of their desire and direction. He needs the feeling of originality that is evidence of the new person that he is, and yet he also needs the feeling of being like others. This dilemma of the child's, like that of the parent, finds its solution in the atmosphere of healthy respect both for the individuality of the child and for the direction the parent is free to give. Asserting and yielding are always relative to each other, both in the parent and in the child. The child who feels the parent's respect for himself gains the courage to be himself. Instead of suffering from his difference, he finds in his own uniqueness the real source of his vitality and creativeness, where he neither exaggerates his difference to prove he is still master of his own destiny nor denies it in the fear of becoming isolated and alone.

Clinical practices designed to help emotionally disturbed children and their parents have been developing a more positive attitude toward both parents and children. It recognizes that the relationship of parents and children itself contains a potential for the very change that is sought when it is decided to use a clinic service. The personnel of our clinics need to acquire the skill to help parents and children through their participation in the services provided, to regain a feeling of responsibility in their relation to each other. The emphasis in our clinics has shifted away from a preoccupation with problems; we now help people having problems to find effective ways to deal with them. In clinical experience we do find parents and children, even those who are quite disturbed and neurotic, able to make effective use of the skill we are trying to ac-

III. Parent — Child

quire and to make available. In clinical experience we are finding more and more support for the basic theme of this discussion, that the parental role provides the most constructive force in the life of a child, and the potential for this positive influence can be recaptured and revitalized even where problems have become serious, if our clinical skills are based on this belief. Both parents and children can then be helped to believe in and to help themselves.

No parent is ever helped by confronting him with his mistakes, by pointing a finger at him and saying: "You are the problem." Many troubled parents know they are involved in the problems of their children—the deeper the involvement, the greater are the defenses set up to disguise this fact. Books and lectures and clinical practice that seek to make them aware of their wrongdoing tend to generate more anxiety and greater need either to project the responsibility on other factors or to feel it so totally that the child is left out as a participant. Neither of these results leads to healthier living. But when our clinical services are based on an interest in and respect for people as we find them and as they present themselves for help, then our clinics do become effective instruments in helping troubled parents and children.

When a child is anxious and confused, he can find in the parent a source of strength. He acts on the truth contained in the Biblical verse: "When my heart is overwhelmed, lead me to the rock that is higher than I."

The parent, with his adult strength, gives the child the support and direction he needs to find his own strength and the courage to reach out for the ever new.

The parent will supply a child with a strength designed, not to overwhelm him, but to provide him with a foundation upon which he can build his own life.

1. How does one handle a child's negative response to a reasonable request when resentment is aroused in the child by punishment?

This is an interesting question because the reasonableness may be in the parent's own feeling about it. The child, however, may react against it. A negative response in a child can be a normal response. We really begin to worry about a child when he is so complacent that he follows every request without any reaction to it of his own. Such a pattern reflects a selfless quality in the child. Equally difficult problems arise when the negative pattern of response becomes dominant and is activated by any request that requires some yielding response.

Where a parent can recognize not only the reasonableness of the request but also whatever reasonableness there may be in the child's negative reaction to it, the request need not be shunted aside. The parent can hold steady to such a request and allow the child to test whether or not he can wipe out certain demands by protesting against them. A child who finds that his negative reaction is respected, but that the parent stands steady against it, as a rule does not develop problems.

As for the resentment aroused in the child by punishment, the youngster's resentment may not be anything to be concerned about. If the parent is able to

III. *Parent — Child*

recognize that he represents a force that legitimately makes certain reasonable requirements of the child, who may put the parent to real tests to make sure he means what he says, it is better to let the child express his feelings. When a parent can respect a child's negative and resentful feelings while holding firm to what is required, the child learns to respect and use that firmness without feeling that he is surrendering himself to a force bigger than himself. There is a great difference between yielding and surrendering. A child has to react negatively before he can feel he is an individual in his own right. Then the yielding can represent a new-found strength in himself.

If parents can respect a child's way of responding, they can avoid an endless type of struggle that can develop in the debate of "You will" with the response "I will not." The child who says and feels "I will not" arouses the anger of the parent and is denied the right even to wish he could change the request. The result is either to intensify the struggle or to create a submissive attitude. Both are bad.

2. **Do you think bottle feeding, which has almost entirely replaced breast feeding, has a deleterious psychological effect on the child? For example, can you trace delinquency to this?**

I should say no to the last half of that question, because the causes of delinquency cannot be traced to any single factor.

If the mother, however, does not breast-feed her child because of indifference to the child's needs, this can represent a negative and resentful attitude of the mother toward her child, and trouble may be brewing. I know in today's culture mothers get a great deal of help in avoiding breast feeding. Some doctors like to help a mother get the child on the bottle as quickly as possible, and breast feeding has gone out of style. I think, however, that it is coming back with a new emphasis and with a new feeling of the mother's responsibility for her child.

There is no question that breast feeding in the early life of an infant is the natural, biological feeding experience and gives the mother the feeling she is fulfilling her natural biological role for a child. The child benefits by this. If breast feeding can be restored in that early period, not because it is the proper thing, but because it is the natural fulfillment of the mother role at that time, then the feeding experience of the child in early life will be more normal.

That does not mean that a child who is bottle-fed can't be a perfectly normal baby, because he can. A mother can convey to a child through bottle feeding the same sense of warmth and friendliness and affection as with breast feeding.

If the feeding of a child, whether from breast or bottle, carries with it a feeling of rejection and a wish that the child never existed, that same attitude will begin to influence all aspects of the mother-child relation and start in motion negative struggles that gradually mount and mount. The end result may be a pattern of delinquency when the child carries on his fight against all forces that make demands upon him.

III. *Parent — Child*

3. How widespread do you believe the Œdipus complex to be?

The only really widespread and universal thing connected with this is the mother-and-child relationship. The mother is a symbol of infancy to a child, and growing up requires constant change in this basic relation. The child has to relinquish the mother, and the mother has the opportunity and responsibility of helping him move out of the closeness required in the infantile period. Many difficulties can arise out of this process.

The important thing for me in the Œdipus analogy is that both mother and child have widely varying degrees of difficulty in this process. The overpossessive mother builds a fence around her relation to a child, and the child may struggle against the demands for separation in growing up. If the child clings to a mother who is also clinging to him, we may expect a lot of turmoil.

The father is involved in this Œdipus situation in an interesting way. If we go back to the Œdipus myth we find it was to the father that the oracle came and said: "You had better watch out. You are going to have a boy who is going to grow up and replace you." That is the original Œdipus myth. The sequence of developments in the Œdipus drama started with the fear aroused in the father.

If we apply the myth literally to modern life we do observe the anxiety some men have about their ability to sustain the father role in the face of a growing child.

There is much more to be said about the Œdipus

analogy, but I have touched on this one aspect which seems pertinent to this discussion.

4. What measures can a mother take to compensate for the early disappearance of the father in the life of a male or female child?

When this happens, the family constellation is thrown out of balance. When the mother can feel the value of what she can be to her child and not feel she has to double and demand of herself that she be everything to her child because of the loss of the father, the difficulties are certainly diminished. Realistically, she can't be two parents.

Take, for example, a family where the father has died. The mother naturally feels a great deficit in her own living; she is denied the adult companionship she had with the father. If she uses the child as a substitute and requires from the child the satisfactions she had from her husband, or if she tries to substitute for the father in the child's life, you can see that a false element will begin to enter the mother-child relationship. But if a mother can feel the value of what she has to give in the face of changed circumstances, a balance can be restored in the new family situation.

The temporary absence of the father during the war created difficult situations for many mothers and children. Where the mother could feel that what she could give to the child right out of herself as the mother, and not as the mother plus the father, was enough, in most instances they managed to get along in a natural and healthy way and to leave a real place in

III. *Parent — Child*   [87

the family for the father when he returned after military service. On the other hand, when the mother tried to be everything to the child, she left very little place for the father when he returned. In such families the return of the father required a much more intense reorganization of the family. This resulted in disturbances for the mother, the child, and the father.

5. What is meant by anal and oral characters?

Let me say just a word on that, but I don't want to get off into technical jargon.

The other day I saw a boy with a severe speech disorder. He is a boy who had never been able to show anger. Feeling anything that is negative reflexly causes a fragmentation of his speech capacity. One day during a therapeutic hour he started to tell me in a most garbled way that he hadn't wanted to come to see me that day.

That would seem like a fairly natural thing for a boy to say, but for this boy to begin to reveal something that was negative and could carry some connotation of hostility led to the most exaggerated kind of speech disorder. When I helped that boy get out into the open that actually what he was trying to tell me was that he wished I was somewhere else so he wouldn't have to come to see me that day, and helped him share that feeling with me, he quickly relaxed and for the next fifteen minutes he was able to talk in a natural way.

It is not accidental that the anal and oral areas of the body are important in the early emotional development of the child. He feels the first physiological discomfort over his need for food. He is restored to a feeling of comfort after being fed. Around mouth activity he feels his first needs and first frustrations when food is not immediately available. Around mouth activity he feels his new relatedness to the mother who satisfies his need. Around the functioning of the oral apparatus he gives expression to first feelings. Being the first anatomical area associated with the expression of feeling, it can and does become the means of channeling the more violent feelings of rage and anger. Later the oral apparatus takes on new functions while retaining the function of taking in food. Through oral activity the child learns to use language to convey meaning, so it is associated closely with developing relationships. These functions are disturbed when a child experiences more feeling than he can master, and they become in some neurotic conditions a bulwark against an open expression of feeling. But this involves a disturbance of the normal functions of speech and the ingestion of food. Familiar expressions such as "I was speechless with rage" convey a psychological truth.

The same process occurs when the child experiences the need to exercise control of the bladder and anal functions. When a child is physiologically ready, the parent begins to require that he take responsibility for these functions and trains him to acquire habits of control. The child feels the impact of the parent's desire and in varying degrees reacts against these requirements. When the negative pattern becomes dominant, these anatomical areas are associated with feelings of the "I will not" type. Struggles begin to focus on these areas and can be closely associated with feelings that cannot be expressed openly. A child meeting the impact of a too demanding habit-training effort will feel

III. Parent — Child   [89

the need to organize himself against these parental efforts to take something away from him.

6. At what age does the infant begin to realize that the mother is not part of himself?

I think that out of his first frustration he begins to get an awareness that he has a need, but that the source of satisfying it is outside himself. That can accelerate the process of differentiation and starts quite early in the life of an infant, within the first few months.

7. How can one overcome the effect of institutionalization on an infant one adopts?

The question is an excellent one, but assumes that all of the effects of institutionalization are deleterious. The most frequently destructive effect is that the child has not had a basic relationship in which to get his start in life.

If parents, in adopting a child who has had no experience with a mother, can really feel a readiness to allow a relationship to develop gradually, the original handicap can be overcome in the natural give-and-take of living.

A great many people who adopt a child and feel and know that the child has had serious deprivations rush in so fast in their great zeal to love the child that they really frighten him and push him away from the very thing they want to give; they set up a roadblock that may be difficult. A child who is seriously deprived can experience emotional indigestion.

Children are participants in the building of a relationship, and many children who have lacked intimacy because of institutional living will need to move rather slowly. They may withhold their positive feelings of love and affection until they can begin to feel their place in their new home.

If the parents can understand and respect that rhythm rather than rushing in and overwhelming the child with affection, this new relationship can grow naturally. The child gets a greater and more enduring sense of security when he has had a real part in building it. The greater the degree of deprivation, the slower will be the process of reaching out to have that need satisfied.

8. How can a mother be helped to give more love and affection to a child who shows great need for more?

Such a parent needs help to bring into the open those feelings which seem to block the natural expressions of love for the child. A common factor in such blocking in a parent grows out of an identification of the child with a quality in themselves or in another which they cannot tolerate. Helping the parent to see the child for what he is can help to unleash more positive feelings toward him. Parents can be helped to face the more negative and hostile feelings they have for a child and find they are not doomed because of those feelings. Parents who can come to grips with those more negative feelings can begin to discover and use the more positive feelings that have been submerged and distrusted. Their efforts to deny and atone for hostile feelings give an artificial quality to

III. *Parent — Child* [91

the love they try to show a child. A more real feeling of affection emerges when they find they can be responsible for and master the other feelings that have blocked them. Denial of feeling is not a very effective way to gain mastery over that feeling.

9. Can indulging a greedy child help him to grow into a normal adult? The child is thirteen and has been and is neurotic.

This child seems to be trying to incorporate into himself everything he can get and to give out very little, like a sponge. I suppose if he can continue to get that kind of indulgence, which in itself is a neurotic pattern, there is very little in life that can really send him off in a different direction. He won't just grow out of it.

If the child reaching the age of thirteen is still having that kind of indulgent relation, we begin to realize that the neurotic pattern isn't merely in the child, but exists in the situation. The persons who indulge the child are an essential part of the neurotic pattern.

10. What is the best method to employ in order to get obedience in a child of three years?

Maybe just to apply some of the principles I have been talking about that concern respecting what you have to give to the child and expecting the child in his fashion to find how he can use what you give.

Obedience is not a virtue in itself. A parent who assumes that obedience to his desire should occur just because he is a parent fails to recognize that obedience in a healthy sense grows out of the give-and-take of living together. Strict obedience for a three-year-old, or for a child at any age, postulates that a child has no right to a choice of action and has no need to react against the parents' will. A three-year-old child is awakening to the reality of having a will of his own and will test out what he can do with it. He needs the strength of a parent to find useful ways of using his own strength. We know the power of a three-year-old to make an adult feel helpless. It can reduce the adult to feeling like a disorganized mass of protoplasm. The child needs the strength of an adult that can stand steady against his testing-out behavior, a strength that does not require the submissiveness of the completely obedient child, but that is not threatened when a child says "I will not" to a reasonable demand.

IV

AGE – YOUTH

by FRANCIS J. BRACELAND, M.D.[1]

MONTAIGNE warns us that we must gently endure the laws of our condition, for we are all fated to become aged. He admonishes us that it is "unseemly to grieve" about that which is adversely affecting everyone else at the same time. The *warning* is concerned with the subject matter of this discussion. The *admonition* can be presently applied by you: if in treating this topic I wander afield, everyone around you will be in the same fix and it will be unseemly for you to grieve.

Interpersonal relationships between youth and old age present numerous facets. With many of them we are familiar, and all of them reflect those conflicts which inevitably infest the core of men's relationships. Some of these facets we should mention before attempting to ferret out the underlying causes and effects, similarities and discrepancies, motivations and inhibitions.

One of the aspects of the problem has to do with the advancing age of the growing population of our country. Statistics indicate that if all other catastrophic forces remain what they now are, in twenty-five years ten per cent or more of the people in these United

[1] Jefferson Medical College. Professor of Psychiatry, Graduate School, University of Minnesota; consulting psychiatrist, Mayo Clinic.

States will have reached or passed the age of sixty-five. There is no doubt of the accuracy of these statistics, but in some of the observations made upon them we detect a suggestion of panic. The observations seem to carry with them unasked and unanswered questions that, to the psychiatrist's mind, might easily be the forerunners of phobic states, of morbid fear.

For one thing, Malthus is resurrected—talk of our plundered planet and our overburdened economic system reappears. For another, fast-working social scientists produce their counterpart of Einstein's famous equation, and people are converted into jobs, jobs into employer-employee contracts. Then by a series of quick computations the whole equation is reduced to dollars and the lugubrious prediction emerges that we can't afford old age. Youth cannot carry such a staggering burden. In this type of thinking the point of departure between youth and age is one of economics, and fear induced in the young engenders hostility to the aged.

From sources less frequently medical than non-medical, moreover, come warnings of the ills to which the elderly are prone: cancer, heart disease, arteriosclerosis and—senility itself. This type of warning reaches a wider audience than the actuary's tables and hence has a greater potentiality for harm. If these alarms are dramatized too vividly, unnecessary fear and worry are added to age, already heavily burdened, and it seeks security at the expense of youth.

Here I am not attacking statements that are scientific and accurate. But dire predictions and ominous overtones too frequently are consequences of failure to appreciate the role that change plays in human affairs. "Among new men, strange faces, other

IV. Age — Youth [95

minds," ² change brings new emphasis and new meanings; it blends what appear to be incompatibles. When Heraclitus pointed out that no man bathes twice in the same stream, he enunciated a dynamic principle that infuses human affairs with healthy life. Pathological states exist in society only when the measured places of time and change are radically altered. As the Preacher in Ecclesiastes taught: "To everything there is a season, and a time to every purpose under the heaven: a time to be born, and a time to die." ³

Realization of the importance of time, then, becomes a prerequisite as we investigate the relationship between youth and age. In this exploration of chronology we may be obliged to deviate from the factual and enter the realm of interpretation. This, in fact, is the duty of the psychiatrist, who deals in human symbols and their meanings. He must interpret the currents and tides of human affairs in terms of their psychological significance to individuals. To him almost nothing is an isolated phenomenon; all things are related in time, and also many hidden things are causes of observed effects. To understand people and their foibles, it is necessary to consider them in their relatedness.

First, then, what are the hallmarks of age as arrogant youth and as "crabbed age" itself identify them? Jonathan Swift, who wrote to a friend: "There is no such thing as a fine old gentleman," enunciated them many years ago, and popular observation and medical science have confirmed them many times since. There is failure of the memory, particularly for recent events. The

² Tennyson: "The Passing of Arthur," line 406.
³ Ecclesiastes iii, 1–2.

five senses become impaired in varying degrees. Moods become rapidly fluctuating and at times inappropriate. Behavior is typified by preoccupation, with its stereotyped defenses. The thought content concerns days gone by.

Said in another fashion: in a manner analogous to the hardening process which renders the blood vessels inelastic as age advances, the avenues by which old people try to effect meaningful communication with the surrounding world are impaired and gradually cut off. The sounds of current events are heard faintly and distantly if at all. Concern is with events long since over. Change or the threat of change evokes an irritable response as the effort is made to keep things as they were. Time is slowing to a stop for the aged as they strive to maintain the status quo. These are yesterday's radicals, now rigid and inflexible in outlook.

"We take a sight at a condition in life," wrote Stevenson, "and say we have studied it; our most elaborate view is no more than an impression. If we had breathing space, we should take the occasion to modify and adjust; but at this breakneck hurry, we are no sooner boys than we are adults, no sooner in love than married or jilted, no sooner one age than we begin to be another, and no sooner in the fulness of manhood than we begin to decline toward the grave. It is in vain to seek for consistency or expect clear and stable views in a medium so perturbed and fleeting." [4]

Even manifestations of age are not all consistent, for man lives, as it were, on two planes. The biological or physical plane is concerned with structure, and the psychological and physiological plane is concerned

[4] R. L. Stevenson: *Crabbed Age and Youth.*

IV. Age — Youth

with function. The aging process affects each plane in a characteristic way. Although the two planes are inextricably intextured and cannot be separated, for our purposes here we shall consider them separately.

We pass quickly over the physical plane, for that is only incidentally germane to this discussion. "Sans teeth, sans eyes, sans taste, sans everything," tells the story. You know it well.

When we move into the realm of function, however, aging assumes a different role and we see it in many forms. Aging is the process brought about by time functionally slowing to zero. There is little change in the direction of growth, but, as has been said, the many arteries of communication that tie the individual to the world about him become clogged and blocked. He is in the world but not of it. Failing in communication with the outside world, he substitutes things as they were. Things as he would like to have them he substitutes for reality brought about by change. People and events are altered without regard for time and its factual insistence. Thus slowly and surely each Mrs. Gummidge is cut off from the stream of life and remains preoccupied with her loneliness and thoughts of "the old 'un."

It is evident now that we have left the world of hard and fast structure and, with the psychiatric license permitted us, we enter the world of distorted function. Therein fullness of years is not a prerequisite to becoming old and we meet the aged child and the aged adolescent as well as the aged person of chronologically middle life. All of these have stopped growing, and when men stop growing, a process begins that eventually equalizes them functionally regardless of age or youth. The young become old; the old become young.

This regression is the infantilization of which the psychiatrist speaks. It is the turning back to an earlier age in time. It is a paradoxical and pathological situation not to be confused with the physiology of orderly sequential growth. Close inspection of the phenomena of regression as displayed at an age earlier than senility would be expected to appear clarifies the relation of these phenomena to the aforementioned reactions of the normally aged. Peculiarly, moreover, personal meanings are given to every event, and the individual reacts with exaggerated and untoward feeling to what, if he were normal, he would accept dispassionately. Inadequate to the demands of everyday life, the individual gradually withdraws; he becomes seclusive and preoccupied with himself. If this state progresses, he needs to be cared for, because, like the truly aged, he becomes "sans everything."

Actually, to determine a patient's relation to time and change is one way of examining the data in a case presenting psychopathological aspects. Man, as Korzybski characterized him, is a "time-bound animal." The nature of his failure to adjust in this regard gives rise to his symptoms. Necessarily the adjustment varies widely. At one extremity of the spectrum are the psychoneurotic maladjustments; at the other end are the psychoses. Each is a way of life, a compromise that the individual makes with himself in relation to others. The psychoneurotic on the whole is more effectual than the psychotic in his adaptation, but each in his own characteristic way has stopped his maturation. Each is held up in time and therefore is attempting to

IV. Age — Youth

effect a rapprochement between two times. One time is the here and now; the other is that hoped-for period in the past or future when things were or will be different. Seen as we have considered the process, this is a kind of aging.

By the same token we can now see that the psychiatrically troubled person is not unique in his difficulties. At one time or other all of us experience some modification of his type of difficulty and we are forced, by this artificially imposed aging, to use the same kind of defense reaction he uses, and the same adaptive mechanism, in order to help in our interpersonal relations.

The normal emotional reaction to aging, seen in this light, is much more understandable than otherwise. The fear of loneliness, of isolation, or of separation from others is the threat implied in this kind of aging. It helps to explain why such a premium is placed on youth. Viewed ideally, youth is assumed to be the time of life when all of the perquisites are given us and few of the responsibilities are required of us. Freedom from responsibility offers the allurement of freedom from anxiety and worry. It promises a minimum of chafing restrictions externally or internally imposed. It is accompanied by the boon of independence incident to its status, and whether or not it is an overpraised season, as Samuel Butler says it is, it holds for persons of old age a widespread attractiveness.

Actually the situation is not so romantic. Only in the eyes of the pathologically aged is the opposite of their unhappy state the one to be desired. In reality their wish is based on chimerical values. The world as we know it does not permit unrestricted freedom without requiring proportionate payment in responsibility.

Instead of total independence, there exists for youth a form of interdependence that grants benefits on a *quid pro quo* basis. Truism or not, the returns are proportionate to one's investment. There is a strict personal audit of emotions; output, therefore, always must balance income if the equilibrium between a man and his fellows in the affairs of the world is to continue. Psychological aging (not to be confused with maturing) at any time of life is a consequence of failure in emotional economics. The methods by which the to-and-fro exchange of feelings is accomplished are not adequate for the job and, to extend the metaphor, emotional bankruptcy ensues.

The problem of mental disease as a consequence of pathological aging is perhaps best presented by mention of some of the conditions for which psychiatrists are consulted daily. Extreme aging of the young is encountered in cases of schizophrenia. Although the final expression of the disease may seem to be an acute reaction that began precipitously, closer investigation reveals that the schizophrenic break is the final expression of a process that has been operative throughout many years of the patient's life. Like aging, it is a developmental phenomenon. The classical hallmarks of aging are all to be found, as they leave telltale marks on the patient's interpersonal relations. The withdrawn, seclusive attitude of nonparticipation walls off the outside world of change so that communication with real people becomes progressively more difficult. The diminishing to-and-fro relations require that if the basic psychological essentials are to be met, there must be an internal substitution for the external lack. In functional terms this is what is responsible for the delusions,

IV. Age — Youth

hallucinations, and illusions that fill the schizophrenic's world with portents and signs reminiscent of the real world of people. When this forward progress in time ceases, regression sets in and the patient lives in phantasied bygone times, striving desperately for love and protection. There are no bounds to the childlike aging of dementia præcox—it is the dementia of young people, "sans everything."

Adolescence presents the problems in interpersonal relationships that it does in our culture because of what seem to be anachronisms in function. There is the great trial of being mature in bodily structure but childlike socially and economically. The stretch of this discrepancy across the years imposes an enormous burden on the qualities of adaptation and conformity. Here is the frustration of a man being held in a boy's job. How shall he act? Which vocal register shall he use? He has several of them. Shall he use the faltering bass of an unsure manhood or the unbecoming contralto of boyhood? How can he be expected to accept all of the responsibilities, constraints, and manifold duties of adult life if he is to have few or none of its privileges?

In the light of this anachronism which all too frequently plagues the youth, it is not difficult to see why his means of communication with his parents and elders become blocked, with resulting imperfections in interpersonal relationships and understanding. In order to carry on meaningful communication with others, one must accept a frame of reference that is at least nearly the same as theirs. But this is difficult if not impossible for the youth dislocated in time. For one thing, he is here and now, though actually he is expected to, and tries to, function in a time gone by. He interprets present-day communications in a frame of reference of long ago. Symbols change or lose meaning, but pathetically he clings to ancient values to which these symbols were once appropriate. A counterpart of this dislocation is encountered in the person lost in the turn the general conversation has taken; he attempts at every opportunity to turn it back to ground with which he is familiar.

This corresponds to the loss of memory of recent events and the preoccupation with the past of the senile. It is a quasi-pathological aging in youth. Obviously it occurs in all shades and degrees. To the degree that it is present it cuts off youth from the reality of people, things, and events about him. The severity or lack of severity of the inevitable regression that turns time around in an effort to equalize the emotional pressure of anachronism ultimately determines the role one plays. To everything there is a season.

There are numerous demonstrations of the fact that regression, with respect to time values, is a distortion that moves one's role and function back to an age when capacities were adequate to tasks. For instance, in infancy communication is fairly circumscribed and unsophisticated. Behavior conveys both meaning and feeling, and for that reason in childhood they are closely allied. It is only as the individual grows and matures that thought, feeling, and behavior take on separateness. When, in response to current stress, a person ages functionally and regresses to an earlier time, there are reflections of his anachronistic adaptation in his thoughts, feelings, and behavior. This is pathological aging; time stands still.

IV. Age — Youth

It is not only in childhood and adolescence that one is vulnerable to premature or pathological aging. All stages of adulthood hold similar perils. The burdens and cares of parenthood, the business of, day in and day out, remaining on the job, the emotional accompaniments of competition, the scramble for social station and prestige, the acceptance of limitations and the failure to realize potentialities, the erosion of personal defenses by births, illness, and deaths of those upon whom we depend, all these and more in the crucible of emotional life are melted down to the insoluble residue of stress. The ratio of stress to time equals the success of adaptation. This is what was cogently observed in Ecclesiastes when the stress of birth and the stress of death were related to time: "A time to plant, and a time to pluck up that which is planted; a time to kill, and a time to heal; a time to destroy, and a time to build; a time to weep, and a time to laugh; a time to mourn, and a time to dance." [5]

There could scarcely be a more comprehensive list of stresses of adult life or a more accurately conceived relationship than those outlined in the chapter from which the verses are quoted. Only if change is not constant, only if time stops, does pathological aging begin, because the ingredients of the well-adjusted life paradoxically absorb all of these stresses, each in its season. Thus it becomes apparent that the secret of successful youth is the secret of keeping things in their season; recognizing them for what they are; accepting the tide of changing events neither with passivity nor with independence, but rather with recognition of the sharing and the relatedness of interdependence. Man,

[5] Ecclesiastes iii, 2–4.

Aristotle pointed out, is a social animal, needing for his daily sustenance and support the food of comradeship, of love, and of belonging. Since pathological aging isolates, it clogs and stops up the channels of life.

The adequacy with which an adult meets these life stresses naturally varies. At some period or other in life, to a greater or lesser degree, each of us has the personal difficulties that ordinarily we assume to be the sole prerogative of the other man. No one is quite facile enough to cope with every stress without some personal conflict. The nature of the expression of this conflict, its type of symptoms in other words, depends on many things. The wide variety of clinical possibilities often is the most serious obstacle to a clear general understanding of the problem of adjustment and maladjustment.

What is more difficult to understand, however, is not that people are unique and individual and that their problems are likely to take on a similar tinge of individuality, but that the ultimate solution of those difficulties is the responsibility of the person possessing them. This has many implications. First, it means that to everyone there is a season of stress. The effect on each person has unique meaning and unique significance for that person. This is why there are no panaceas. This is why no single prescription for happiness and content can be compounded and taken with equal promise of good results for everyone. This is why one learns only from personal experience and why it is that examples and precepts plus illustrative cases are of such limited personal value to us. This is why learning by doing is axiomatic. This is why the language for communicating, as poets and writers have

IV. Age — Youth

long since discovered, is so difficult to acquire. This is why age has so much difficulty in trying to pass ready-made and second-hand experiences, hard come by, on to youth. This is why fathers, however sacrificing, cannot spare their sons the full measure of stress that constitutes life in its seasons.

Time and again psychiatrists and others interested in the problems of youth and old age are importuned for answers: "Tell us how to open the channels of communication among people! How can we put an end to the isolationism of pathological aging? How can we stay young in heart?"

These questions have been asked by many people in many generations. The search for the fountain of eternal youth has been an intriguing but disappointing quest. Many false prophets have thought, as Ponce de León thought, that *the* answer lay in things of the physical world—nectars, elixirs, unguents, lotions, baths, spas, and the like. In their season each has had a vogue: mandrake, hellebore, goat glands, and synthetic endocrines. Each in time has had its devotees whose task, as they saw it, was to convince an aging civilization that here was the answer to its problems. However scientific, however biologically potent, these agents do not satisfy the functional wants of aging with which we are occupied.

Of recent years much has been said of the use of powerful hormonal concentrates in treatment of the psychological consequences of pathological aging. Menopause is no longer sex-linked, say the proponents of the latest "what is it," the male menopause. The troubles of middle life for both male and female lie in their waning biologic capacities, proclivities, and capabilities. The barrage is directed against that doleful period, the "change of life" (a term that in itself is enough to depress one), as if all life was not change. If an aberrant biologic process is the cause, the remedy allegedly awaits the time when sufficiently potent ingredients for replacement or substitution therapy are at hand, so the reasoning goes, and that time is now.

There it is: the frenetic attempt to treat with gland substances the pathological aspects of psychological aging. The outcome is foredoomed because of failure to appreciate the underlying dynamics responsible for the blocked lines of communication. The depression, tension, agitation, restless discontent; the hopelessness and helplessness; the self-accusation and self-incrimination; the sense of desolation; the inability to concentrate on or be interested in the present; the weariness and desire to quit this life—all of these are the complaints of the pathologically aged melancholic. He exemplifies the paradox of the alive but not living. His condition is the extreme of a class of disturbances, many of which are less severe; their number is legion. Here is the anachronism that a former generation called the "middle-aged flapper" and here the man who (with a wink) is old, but "has young ideas." Here is the psychosocial tragedy, the May-December marriage.

One can get an idea of the widespread distribution of articles that "restore youth" by reading the advertisements of the purveyors of these trappings. This is neither the time nor the place for a sociological investigation of them. Suffice it to say that they cover a range of things that (a) preserve or restore the hair (a sure sign of youth) or (b) keep bulges where youth de-

IV. *Age — Youth*

mands they should be, or keep other organs or parts from the inroads and ravage of age. Were such activities merely limited to commerce, it would not be too distressing, for one is not compelled to buy them. The unhappy circumstance is that there are overtones that to those of us seriously concerned with the problems of youth and old age are indications of significant social attitudes, values, and trends. The implications are that old age, with the specters of disability, disuse, and death in the background, is something to fear, shun, and avoid mentioning. Children are admonished never to ask anyone his age for fear of embarrassing him. The cult of "over twenty-one" is upon us. At the same time children are warned to be (or act) their age, which means to grow up—while social custom almost requires adults to act younger than their age. The connotations of the epithet "the old man" are obvious. By general acceptance and by custom he is assumed to be irascible, crotchety, unyielding, ungrateful, and unregenerate. He is the prototype of pathological aging. The significant point here is that age is being made a scapegoat.

We have sufficient understanding of the psychopathology of "scapegoatism" to know that the hostility herein expressed and converted toward the unhappy object is born of earlier and deeper psychological conflict than is revealed on superficial examination. In this instance it is an indication of already defective avenues of communication in our society. Youth is fair-haired and old age "sans hair," figuratively as well as actually, because of a misunderstanding of their respective roles. The role of one is to be sought and preserved by every means. It is the hero's role and classically he is young, handsome, and capable. The other role is the villain's; craftiness, tyranny, and lust for power are the personality requisites. The characterization continues: one is radical, the other conservative; one is generous, the other selfish, and so on. The list of these antithetical qualities could be, and actually has been, extended in the stereotypes of our social thinking as well as in our literature.

Basically, the existence of these attitudes is an indication of a psychological failure in intrapersonal and interpersonal relationships. In a gross way, the problems of the individual and the problems of the group are reciprocal and interdependent. Society with its customs, traditions, and culture is the persisting amalgam of the thought, feeling, and behavior of its members, accumulated over a long time. Like the mind and body relationship, neither one came first. Each bears a reciprocal functional relationship to the other. Crystallized in the culture of a society are those various states and relationships which in the individual change too rapidly to be fully appreciated. Culture is a structure of interrelationships and values and attitudes built by the members of a society. Social pathology in its broadest sense is akin to pathological aging in individuals. Not only this, but also social pathology contributes to, and is reflected in, the disrupted function of its individual members. The final test of adjustment can be only the quality of the adaptation that is made.

The inability of a society to establish safeguards and self-correctives that will allow it to change continually in accordance with the demands imposed upon

IV. Age — Youth

it cannot fail to affect adversely the total function of its members. Social institutions are the jelled expression of attitudes and values. Obviously they have a difficult time of it. On the one hand there is the necessity of maintaining sufficient fixity to avoid the chaos of the amorphous. On the other hand there is the necessity of adequately reflecting in altered demands the needs of its human members. Unhappily, in the best-ordered societies there is always a cultural lag, a slow social responsiveness to individual needs.

In a measure the problem of better planning reflects this cultural lag. We have only recently come to realize that the market place reflects values, sentiments, and attitudes created elsewhere. Thus it is that here also old age has become separated from chronology. We have the social paradox of the old men, unemployable at forty except in time of war; the fixed and arbitrary retirement ceilings which assume that all contributing usefulness stops at sixty or sixty-five years; the failure of industry to be psychologically prepared for, much less psychologically able to accept, this newly created social institution of old-age-by-fiat.

From the psychiatrist's standpoint catastrophe always follows a capricious and arbitrary deprivation of necessary defense. The social and personal problem of old age in our culture shows our collective penchant for precipitating catastrophe. For example, with old age made as lowly a state as it is generally, there develop all the social and psychological defenses against it to which I have alluded. The fact of it is carefully shielded behind such grisly euphemisms as the already mentioned "over twenty-one," "seventy years young," "old enough to know better," and such harmless cliches as "life begins at forty," "you too can stay young with the help of . . ." and so forth. These phrases are tacit evidence of the psychological ambivalence with which this time of life is treated culturally with typical disregard for established values. In the so-called hard, practical, common-sense world of facts each one of us becomes old by fiat. We have nothing to say about it and we can do nothing about it except accept it gracefully. We are retired, pensioned, given a dinner and a button, and removed from the vast network of interpersonal relations that have for many years been the grist of our everyday life. Perhaps the action is not so precipitate or indeed so overt for some, but by a kind of social attrition most of us in our present culture are made to feel interlopers and out of tune with a place we felt rightfully ours. The same situation too frequently obtains at home in relation to children. Close on the heels of these threats come insecurity, isolation, and emotional tension. If it is true that a man is as old as he feels, this state of affairs is a most conducive factor to aging.

What are the solutions? Obviously they are many and complex. Observations in the field of child growth and development indicate that indeed the child is father of the man. The education of the child to accept obligations and responsibilities along with rights and privileges is bound to change materially the pattern of nonacceptance which is our attitude toward old age. Security must first be established in the person on a generic basis before its lack on a specific basis can be remedied

IV. Age — Youth

We live in a complex maze of interpersonal relations. They range from the singular on a vis-à-vis basis to the multiple on a distantly related group basis. The interrelationships defy any simple analysis that attempts to keep one facet as the variable to be controlled, changed, or regulated while keeping all others constant. The first step in any attempt to solve the pathology that blights human relations is to see the problems.

Possibly Francis Bacon, nearly four centuries ago, took matters properly in turn. He wrote: "Young men, in the conduct and manage of actions, embrace more than they can hold; stir more than they can quiet; fly to the end, without consideration of the means and degrees; pursue some few principles which they have chanced upon absurdly; care not to innovate, which draws unknown inconveniences; use extreme remedies at first; and that, which doubleth all errors, will not acknowledge or retract them, like an unready horse, that will neither stop nor turn. Men of age object too much, consult too long, adventure too little, repent too soon, and seldom drive business home to the full period, but content themselves with a mediocrity of success. Certainly it is good to compound employments of both; for that will be good for the present, because the virtues of either age may correct the defects of both."[6]

1. Isn't the problem of aging the problem of the American who is afraid of middle age—let alone old age?

That is, might we not well remember the veneration

---
[6] Francis Bacon: "Of Youth and Age."

of the Chinese for age and the common-sense acceptance of Europeans of the same?

Yes, quite. In the primitive cultures the older people seemed to have the better of it. They at least were thought to have acquired wisdom with the years. There is a sensible median between those cultures which neglected and deserted their aged, on one hand, and the Chinese, who venerated them simply because they were old.

Even in our own earlier history our older folks had a place, for the males had frequently a technical knowledge and experience and the woman a domestic knowledge which were useful. Advances in our technical knowledge and our urban civilizations have even minimized these contributions of the elderly. The old folks have even given way to sitters. The fact that old age has come to be equated with uselessness and dependence in our culture probably helps to account for the fear of it. Loss of centrality of position and loss of occupational and social status, and so on, all loom larger than they should. Instead of accepting this period of life as a natural one and preparing for it in time, there is a struggle to hold prerogatives that have been invested with a disproportionate importance, hence the disquiet as old age approaches. It is the accompaniment of a materialistic civilization.

2. **How can women best help themselves in middle age?**

I think one thing that distresses women about middle age is the thought that something is

IV. *Age — Youth*

happening to them which they are unable to do anything about. They are undergoing changes that symbolize the beginning of the end and herald the approach of old age. They have heard of the accompaniments of the menopause in others who have had difficulty and they invest these natural endocrinological changes with an importance that is not inherent in them. They simply signify the end of the childbearing period.

A woman can help herself best in middle age by keeping active and adjusting to whatever changes her external circumstances require. We see many people now whose trouble stems from the fact that they need to be needed. The children have grown and married; the husband is busy; and there is no one for them to fuss over. This signifies uselessness to them because they are unable to transfer that localized usefulness to broader spheres, such as the community, and so on. There is always a place for them in church, social, or community work.

To answer the question succinctly, I should say that the first thing necessary is to approach this age just like any other one. It is a period one inevitably goes through if she lives long enough. It carries no stigma or particular hazard in its wake, so that absence from fear, a desire to keep active and to serve, a willingness to keep going and to keep learning, would obviate most of the difficulty associated with middle age.

3. Do you believe the ideal place for an old person unable to take care of himself is with his children? If yes, how can this arrangement be happier than it often is?

I believe that the older person unable to take care of himself ordinarily will be happier with his children. Whether or not they are happy with him is another story. Much depends on the economic and cultural circumstances of the family. If it were possible for the family to have a place for the parent near by or in the same building but ensuring some privacy for both of them, this might be the best answer to the problem. Unfortunately, the economic and housing situation often precludes this possibility, and a large majority of the older-age group is dependent.

There is no doubt at all that both family and aged dependent need some respite from one another. While those advanced in years frequently try not to interfere in family affairs, they do not always succeed. The children, on their part, try not to be resentful, but they are not always successful and someone gets hurt feelings.

It would ease the situation if arrangements could be made for the parent to visit other relatives or get a short vacation by means of funds contributed by all. It would also help to encourage parents to visit friends and to attend movies, or to have a radio or television of their own, and in their own room if feasible. For the rest I am unable to generalize. Each situation is a specific problem and unfortunately our culture offers little help in the general over-all picture.

IV. Age — Youth

4. How can you help someone whom you see slipping into pathologic aging?

If the process has not gone too far, one frequently can get help. First it is necessary to have a very careful and complete physical and neurological examination. Often the acute symptoms that arise are due to toxicity, poor hygiene, bad eating-habits, or poor elimination. Foci of infection should be sought and eliminated. After one is satisfied that the individual's physical condition is taken care of, an effort should be made to socialize the individual and keep him from isolating himself. If he is mildly depressed, this can be aided medically. Every effort should be made to re-awaken old interests and hobbies. Everything possible must be done to give the patient a new lease on life, and this can be aided by making him feel useful and wanted.

5. How do you account for the emphasis on youth in our economic life? Jobs are denied to older men, yet politically old men are considered valuable.

Perfectly true. In industry we deny a man a job who is sixty-five, and yet we elect him to the Supreme Court, or we elect him to the Presidency of the United States. And it is altogether unexplainable.

People in their later ages are not altogether free from blame in this regard. Employers and personnel managers will tell you, for instance, that a middle-aged or elderly woman whom they employ believing she might do the job can cause a good deal of trouble by wearing the lost cap of office, as it were, by referring constantly to the things that she used to be capable of and used to have, while she looks down a little on the younger girls who are working with her.

It is my belief that as we grow up a little more psychologically, we shall be able to take care of people in older-age groups and give them jobs. For instance, during the war men who had been retired suddenly found that they were most valuable for a period of four or five years. Then when the war was over they had to go back to the innocuous state from which they emerged.

Obviously this is a mistake, just as obviously as it is a mistake to retire a person at sixty-five or sixty-four or sixty-two. It ought to be left open on both ends, because many a man who knows he is going to be retired at sixty-five is of very little use after sixty-three or sixty-two, for this so-called calendar neurosis, this time neurosis as he marks off each succeeding year, weighs heavily upon him.

It should be possible to have some sort of board of management and consultants which would keep people on duty but cut down the hours of work, cut down the arduous tasks, and so on. It should also be possible to give some of those in the older-age groups jobs if their capabilities were carefully looked into. They have great economic importance, and I think this being-old-by-fiat that I spoke of is a terrific waste. I think it certainly makes people fear the onset of each year and leads to the insecurity that distresses them and often makes them sick.

I cannot account for it, except that, from the standpoint of human engineering or of employer-employee

IV. Age — Youth

relationships, we have not grown up. It is certainly paradoxical, as this question points out, that we will not give a man a job and yet will elect him to some of the highest judicial offices in the land.

6. How can the older person keep his personal relations adjusted when he knows his children don't want him around? Isn't it better to retire to books, and the like?

Part of this difficulty is due to the older person's unwillingness to let go of the reins he once held and to realize that children who have grown up are entitled to a life of their own. In this life, of course, should be included regard and respect for the older members of the family and economic assistance if required. It does not, however, include submission.

The older person is at fault when he or she expects to occupy the role he once did or selfishly to demand the constant attention of children whose interests lie elsewhere. If older people become aggressive or demanding, it stirs up resentment. If they assume a role of martyrdom or a "just throw me a bone" attitude, they become nuisances. The attention of older folks should be called to the fact that there are interests in life for people of their age group which contain much more satisfaction and fewer possibilities of danger than a suffocating, interfering relationship with their children.

It is as necessary for the parent to cut his end of the silver cord of emotional dependence as it is for the child. Parents must develop satisfactory emotional relationships and keep their lines of communication open; otherwise they are fated to slip backward. Retiring to books and similar interests has a place, of course. It is part of the picture we have of the serenity of age, when we hope to have time to read things we have always wanted to read. Our attitude has to be right, however, for if we retire in pique, we shall get depressed.

7. What is the prognosis of these psychopathological cases at the so-called change of life, menopause?

It is as I told you before. Fear of the menopause is a bogy. This period of life is a natural and normal one—just as normal as was puberty in adolescence. We now know that the disease "involutional melancholia" can be cleared up symptomatically in a matter of weeks by the newer psychiatric therapies.

The idea is not to wait until people become depressed and agitated. The illness should be watched for and preventive methods undertaken. The best preventive is to learn adaptability early in the adult years, and acceptance of what cannot be changed.

Before the advent of present-day psychiatric therapy the prognosis of the disease was not very encouraging. The patients remained ill for from eight months to three years. Only fifty per cent of them recovered; the remaining fifty per cent went on to chronic illness or to self-destruction. Now the recovery rate is over ninety per cent and in a much shorter period.

IV. Age — Youth

8. Should older people be urged to keep up with the world or should they be left to their own patterns?

They have to keep up, but must develop their own pattern of so doing. One thing is certain, the world will not adapt to them; so it is only wisdom to adapt to it in ways that are in keeping with their station in life. Instead of urging them to keep up with current events, the trend has been to push them to the background and to leave them to the defeatism to which they have become accustomed. I am sure that the feeling of usefulness and of having a place in the scheme of things is just as important to them as is economic security.

The emotional aspects of growing old have received too little attention. Older people are oversensitive to slights because they are conditioned to them by their own insecurity. They stand upon the few prerogatives remaining to them, while their loneliness and increasing isolation lead to a mild or moderate depressiveness. They see their cronies depart one by one; perhaps their own partner dies and they have little reason to go on themselves. Their aches and pains, usually small and annoying, are taken for granted and they find little real sympathy from the younger generation. Small wonder they do not long survive their partners. Sometimes they seem to have just quit, for under the impact of emotional stress they succumb to diseases that previously they had been able to live with. Their lot is not particularly pleasant in our culture, and you can see that anything that will keep them interested in the outside world is of therapeutic value.

V

RACE MAJORITY – RACE MINORITY

by MARGARET MEAD, PH.D.[1]

WHEN I looked at the topic that I was given in this series and compared it with other topics which dealt with husbands and wives, and parents and children, I wondered a little whether I was assigned this particular subject because race always belongs to the anthropologist or whether there was an implication that there was something in minority-majority relations that there wasn't in husband-wife relations. Perhaps the implication of that question will give us a good starting-point.

Now, majority-minority relations (and "majority-minority" I take to mean that we are just using the current euphemisms, in which you call the group you are rude to a minority, and any group you are polite to, a majority) are something that, so far as is known, has absolutely nothing to do with numbers. There are a great many people in the United States who are willing to prove to you up to the hilt that women are a minority group in this country. I have read one thesis by an undergraduate that proved it in great detail. They have every single characteristic of a minority group except, of course, that they aren't numerically a minority.

[1] Columbia. Associate Curator of Ethnology, American Museum of Natural History.

V. Race Majority — Race Minority

So I am assuming that what we are talking about are relationships between any two groups in the population, one of which thinks it is better than the other, regardless of whether the other agrees or not. You know there are both kinds. There are the minority-majority positions where each group feels infinitely superior to the other. Canada is a good example of this. It is very difficult to use the word *Canadian* in Canada because the French Canadians think it describes *them*, and the English Canadians think it describes *them*. You can't use the word *Canadian* without an adjective before it. I have been in a good many places in Canada where it is better not to use the noun *Canadian* because it is too compromising to someone, usually the speaker, and we have of course the same situation between Catholic groups and Protestant groups, and between different racial groups in different parts of the world.

Which group is up and which group is down, or whether there are two groups each of which thinks it is up and the other is down, does not really matter seriously when you start to define the whole problem.

An anthropologist is always supposed to go back to the beginning in discussing any problem of this sort, and so before I can talk about existing conditions in this country I have to make a few remarks about primitive man. We may assume that the earliest difference recognized in society was between males and females. We know of no society where it has not been regarded as useful to teach little boys that they were little boys, and to teach little girls that they were little girls.

Some societies do it earlier than others. Some insist

on dressing the children differently from birth or naming them differently, and of course some societies teach negatively, teaching little boys that they are not little girls, and little girls that they are not little boys. There is an enormous difference between this approach and that which teaches little boys that they are little boys, and little girls that they are little girls, because if the main thing the little boy is taught is that he is not a little girl but that he might be if he behaved in this fashion or that fashion, he will spend a large part of his life proving to himself and to other people that he is not a female. If he goes head-hunting, he goes not because he likes head-hunting, which can be a perfectly good and up-and-coming sport, but to prove that he is not a female. And a great amount of his effort is spent making sure himself and convincing everybody else that he is not a female.

You can find the same thing in women, of course, too. You find societies where women spend a great deal of their time and effort proving that they are not males. Fainting used to be one of the ways. It has been given up in this country. Blushing used to be one of the ways. That has also virtually been given up; and now there are children of ten in this country who have never even heard the word *blush*. So that both males and females in every society have to spend quite a little time and energy demonstrating that they are themselves, or not the other sex.

That gives you in a sense the basic diagram for majority-minority relations of any sort, because the first important difference that a child learns about is difference in sex, and the second important difference children learn—I don't want to make an absolute state-

V. Race Majority — Race Minority

ment here, for some may learn one before the other—is a difference in size.

In every society children have to learn that they are children, that they are little and other people are big, and they learn this in a variety of ways. They may learn it by being told: "You're nothing but a child. You mustn't open your mouth. You mustn't talk. Children don't talk. Children are seen and not heard"—in which case they may learn to disparage the status of childhood and to want violently to grow up—and silence other children in their turn.

Or they may be taught: "These are the best years of your life, and I don't want to see them clouded, darling." In that case they learn that childhood is the best period of a lifetime and wish to heaven they would never grow up; or when they do grow up, they spend their summer vacations singing songs of their high-school days.

So that on as simple a point as age, again, it is possible to handle the lower position positively or negatively. Either position may be lower; you can be born high and go down, or you can be born low and go up—there is no absolute position at all. Eskimo children speak with the voice of the gods, and the older they get, the less of the gods there is in them. That is true of the Balinese children. They are born very close to heaven and the incorruptible things they say as a baby are from the gods. They go down steadily from that point to middle age, when they are at an all-time low, and then they start climbing again toward heaven. A Balinese gets older and older, and if he gets old enough he is very close to heaven. Then he is back as he was when he was a baby, again trailing a little heaven.

Which part of age is handled as a plus and which is handled as a minus is again a matter of social definition. Children may learn to believe it is good to be big or good to be little or good to be adolescent.

These are two basic sets of categories, and every human being has to learn them. Every society makes it necessary to learn them in some sort of way. The anthropological problem is to define how they do it, to describe the process and what it means to each person. The psychiatric problem is the penalties that people pay for negative definitions of their position, and we have no word for the opposite of the psychiatric approach—positive definitions. Education ought to have been the opposite, but it has got lost, so that at present *psychiatric* tends to mean everything that goes wrong and everything that is especially interesting in the human psyche. Education tends to mean the normal. There is no word for the plusses. There is nobody in the community, no profession, whose job it is to deal with the extra-gifted, the extra-fortunate people who instead of being traumatized by what has happened to them have had seven good things happen to them in a row.

We have our three problems, then: the general anthropological description of the way any society sets up relations between different groups of people (you find the differences); and the psychiatric problem of the prices that people pay through maladjustment, in fear and in anxiety, in cultures where there are negative definitions; and the problem of the plus positions that are offered to people in any society which does not define any human position negatively.

We might begin to explore these problems by con-

V. *Race Majority — Race Minority* [125

sidering first what is close to us: a few questions of how we handle ordinary minority-majority positions in this country in bringing up children. There is hardly a group in this country that doesn't bring up its children by telling them not to behave like other people's children. If they are a nice middle-class family, they tell the children not to behave like those so-and-so's down the street: "You look like a little so-and-so. Go comb your hair. Everybody'll think you are one of them." And "them" can be any group of current immigrants or people of another economic group, or another race who don't have nice middle-class standards and don't comb their hair so often.

At the same time that this is going on in the homes where these nice children are being reared, the children in the other group are being taught: "Well, who do you think you are! Look at her, all dressed up as if she lived up on Center Street." And the behavior of the first group is again being used in part negatively on the children of that group which has been disparaged by the first group.

I think almost everybody can go back over his childhood and remember his mother's instruction. It was filled with admonitions about the language the children shouldn't have used, the manners they shouldn't have had, the jokes they should not have told, the songs they should not have sung, and the things they should not have done on Sunday or in Lent, because to do so made them like some other, less approved people.

Each group uses the behavior, the manners, the style of the other group to bring up its own children. If they were brought up in a Jewish family, they were told when they were stupid that they had a *"goyische kopf*," which I will translate for those who are not erudite: it means having a dumb gentile head. Now, when a Jewish mother is sad because her child has a *goyische kopf*, for instance, she isn't interested in doing anything to the gentiles. She is just awfully bored with her child's lack of brains and wishes it were different. And if the gentile mother finds that her child is paying too much attention to money and is being too sharp, and the gentile stereotype about the Jews is that they are more interested in money than the gentiles are, and are much better at it, she tells the child not to behave as if he were a little Jew. She isn't interested in doing anything to the Jews, but is simply interested in her child.

Both groups are interested in their own children and are trying to bring them up like themselves, which of course is the ideal. They invoke the other group simply as a way of bringing up their children, and the great bulk of prejudice that is built up in any community against any group is there simply because it is an educational device of the average mother to bring up her children by negative reference to disallowed groups.

Perhaps it is: "Don't talk bad grammar, you sound like an immigrant!" I don't know whether or not people today are told they sound like refugees, but I caught myself in one of these bits of parental use of prejudiced remarks. My three-year-old child came out with a little scarf around her head, and I caught myself saying: "You look like a little immigrant!" I wasn't bringing her up; I was just commenting. And a fourteen-year-old said: "But she's not an immigrant, she's a refugee."

V. Race Majority — Race Minority

The word *immigrant* had got moved, you see. Immigrants are people who came to this country a long while ago, in this girl's idea, for economic reasons; refugees are people who came for political and religious reasons, and there is quite a difference between them. In this girl's opinion nobody comes here any more for economic reasons; now the group that wear shawls around their heads are refugees.

When these scarfs worn around the head became popular, as they have become in the last couple of years, they created dreadful problems in the families of actual immigrants. Do you want your daughter to look the way your daughter didn't like you to look five years before? That was five years before it became fashionable to wear a scarf. Then when mothers went around in them, the daughter would say: "Mom, I wish you would get a decent hat and not look like that!" Now the position is reversed because of the style. So that continually, in the definition of the self, the definition of other people is invoked negatively.

I tried to think back over my own upbringing. First I thought that my family were singularly free of most of the stereotypes until I remembered one of my grandmothers used to say, when I didn't comb my hair: "Come and get your hair combed. You look like the wild man of Borneo!" She probably thought the remark was quite safe, and that she wasn't planting any prejudice in me, because she didn't know anything about my future career at all.

Now, in this building of the image of the self by using negative images, the primary negative images are sex and age images. Almost every society brings up a boy to be a boy by telling him not to look like a girl.

Some societies tell girls not to be like boys. Adults are told not to behave like children in almost every society.

This in turn helps to bring up a positive image, because whenever a boy is not behaving like a girl he feels pleased with himself. The behavior may be swearing, shouting, stamping, not crying, not showing emotion, or showing more emotion; it just depends on which society he lives in. But every time he betrays or exhibits behavior that is labeled not that of the other sex, he feels pleased.

I imagine there are quite a lot of gentiles who have been brought up on comments about interest in money being Jewish, who feel awfully pleased every time they don't count their change, and they go all over the place not counting their change and feeling superior. And there is a certain amount of positiveness in the feeling. You see, they feel: "This is what Mother told me to be, not to be like them. All right, I'm not being like them. I'm being what Mother told me to be, I'm being myself."

So in every society that has rank, children have to be taught not to be like the people of lower rank. What is the definition of rank? It is having different manners, different standards from "them" in the lower rank. In the United States, of course, we don't have rank, we have "background." But it adds up to the same thing. We have, of course, family rank. People are brought up to be members of particular illustrious families with particular family traditions: "Our family doesn't do this. These are things that are done by the Smiths and the Joneses, but not by us"—which creates again a sort of rank. You can't define the best family without having less good families to define it by.

V. Race Majority — Race Minority

You may have very sharp contrasts in the way this is done. For instance, in real caste societies, the sort one gets under Hinduism, each caste is the keeper of its own position. If you are a Brahmin and are defiled by the shadow of a low-caste person falling on you, you have to go and spend perhaps a hundred dollars getting pure. This puts a great deal of power in the hands of the low-caste person or group, which they use, and use up to the hilt.

One of the mistakes we make very often in thinking about a caste society like India's is that we fail to realize that the lower castes have enormous power, because upper-caste persons are so clean, so pure, they can do almost nothing for themselves; and unless there are enough lower-caste persons to sweep up and clean and take the garbage out, they can't continue to exist. They are held completely in the grip of their own purity, which they have to spend time looking after and paying other people to look after.

So that at every point the upper caste, the upper-rank group, pays somewhat for the privilege of being themselves, for the privilege of not working with their hands or not carrying a load on the street. There are some societies in which people of high rank cannot carry things; things have to be carried for them. In one primitive society I have visited I could not carry a piece of paper through the village. If I had done so, I should have been so disqualified for entering the houses of the chiefs that I should never have got in at all. Every time I moved around I had to have a little girl walk behind me to carry even the smallest thing. I never was left alone for a minute—which is again one of the penalties of a superior position. You are likely to be steadily surrounded by people who are defined as inferior.

When one reads of India's treatment of its outcastes it seems an appalling denial of full humanity that people can be regarded as so impure that the very falling of their shadow upon a member of a higher caste is misfortune. Nevertheless, in any discussion of majority-minority relations in such a society it is important to realize that the person on whom the shadow may fall is also paying a price—must be always alert, always aware. In some societies the group that is defined as being at the bottom is the freest, because it is the only group that doesn't have to keep up face, the only one that doesn't have to be busy not behaving like some other group.

In a real caste society you can go down, but you can't go up. That means the only people who can relax are already down. That is true in almost any caste position, including our own American South. There is a sort of freedom at the bottom of the system that there isn't anywhere else, because at all other levels people are busy not falling, not behaving like "them," not being classified with "those people."

If one turns for a minute to the strength positions in the societies that are handling differences positively, you get quite a different sort of picture. They simply say to a boy: "You are a boy. You're handsome. You're strong! M-m-m-m-m, you're a boy!"—and never mention girls at all. Then they say to a girl: "Pretty, pretty, pretty, pretty." A girl grows up to expect that she is the kind of creature who will evoke from other people the soft sweet adjectives that are never used for men, that are used only for her, that belong to her and are

V. Race Majority — Race Minority

her right, she is "pretty!" And the boy grows up to think that just because he is a boy, he is handsome, he will be called handsome, he will rate the adjectives that go with "handsome." In such a society you don't have to worry much. It hasn't occurred to the people in it that boys could be girls, or girls could be boys. They think: "There they are," and that is all settled.

There are also certain societies with almost no class differences. We used to have that in certain parts of rural America, where the Joneses were *that* kind of people—the Joneses were the kind of people who kept their fences mended, and they liked book agents and always asked them to dinner, and they always liked to have the preacher on Sunday. "Grandma always had extra room at her table. Mom always did too, and I'm also going to set an extra place."

But that comment didn't include those Smiths down the road who never had the preacher. It was a positive statement. They were the kind of people, the Joneses were, who liked to ask people in. And Mrs. Smith would say: "Dear, dear, I don't know how the Joneses do it. All those children, and Mrs. Jones always asks every Tom, Dick, and Harry to stay to dinner. Don't know how she manages. You know, we're the kind of family that keeps ourselves to ourselves. Always have been. And they used to say that about Grandfather Lacey. He used to keep himself to himself. And I take after him. And I guess most of my children do, too, except Jimmie. He's always running around after a lot of people. I guess when he grows up he'll be more like a Jones."

That gives Jimmie a great deal of leeway. He doesn't have to be like Grandfather Lacey, or like his Mother

Smith, either. His brothers and sisters are, and that's the way it is. And the mother might add: "What he'll probably be, he'll even be a gambler, he'll take to gambling. People that are too friendly with other people, and things like that, they're out at the races." If she says this to Jimmie, then she has undone what she was doing before. "You're going to be that kind of person," even if the Joneses don't gamble. But if she tells him he's not like a Smith, that he doesn't keep himself to himself, and that makes for gambling, she will plant a certain amount of worry in Jimmie's head and he will not be sure whether he ought to be a Smith and keep himself to himself, or whether otherwise he may become a big gambler.

So that in every term that a family uses to define its position, even as Smiths or Joneses, it defines the others positively or defines them negatively. It may equip the child with a sense that he may fail his family, he may not behave like a Jones, and if he doesn't behave like a Jones he's finished; or it may give him such a fear of the Smiths' almightiness that for the rest of his life he has to go around looking everybody over. And anybody he meets he looks over very carefully to see if he acts like a Jones before he can consort with him.

You perhaps think that I am constantly bringing this back to simple family points and not facing the major issues, but the big differences that exist in any society, like our own between the foreign-born and the native-born, or between Protestants and Catholics, or between classes, or between the three races, are all originally worked out in the home and in the child's sense that either who it is or what it is consists in not

V. Race Majority — Race Minority

being some other things, or who it is and what it is consists in being itself. Every one of those differences can be traced back to the home.

A most interesting psychological study was done in California by Sanford and Brunswik [2] over the last three or four years. They gave a large mixed sample of people what we call a shotgun questionnaire. They asked them a lot of questions about how they felt about all kinds of things—every minority group, labor, women, all the different races and religions. If the person questioned was a Protestant, they asked him questions about Catholics, and if he was a Catholic, they asked him questions about Protestants.

The questionnaire was set up to show which people were anti-minority and which people were very pro-minority on positions of any kind. It included such questions as: "Do you think that Negro workers get a fair deal?" and "Do you think they should?" and so on and so forth, so that you could figure out who were the pros and who were the antis.

They didn't bother with the middle people, who are, in a sense, the most important people in any society because there are more of them. In any society that has a division between the foreign-born and the native-born, between English-speaking and non-English-speaking, between Catholic and Protestant, most people do not pay much attention, but merely carry on the

---

[2] Else Frenkel-Brunswik and R. Nevitt Sanford: "Some Personality Factors in Anti-Semitism," *Journal of Psychology*, XX (1945), 271–91. For a final report on this study see T. W. Adorno, Else Frenkel-Brunswik, Daniel J. Levinson, and R. Nevitt Sanford: *The Authoritarian Personality* (New York: Harper & Brothers; 1950).

stereotypes. Whatever the stereotypes may be—whether bringing up children not to behave like the others, or not to marry the others, or not to stick their tongues out like the others—they are all carried on by this large middle group of people. But there is a narrow band at each end of the statistical grouping who were regarded as the significant people for purposes of this California study. The general assumption that those conducting the study worked on was that people may change one way or the other. Then they took the people at the top end of the questionnaire and got mixed up in using the terms *high* and *low*, which is a very good example of what happens in this whole discussion. They called the people who showed most prejudice, for instance, the "*high* anti-Semites." I objected to using an upper-level word for a disapproved idea, but they said: "They showed more of it."

They studied these people who showed most prejudice and then they took the people who showed the most pro-minority feeling, who were described as being at the bottom. They were low on the scale and they held the noble sentiments; the other people were described as high on the scale and they had all the ignoble sentiments. They then studied these two groups of people in great detail, gave them psychiatric interviews and apperception tests and all sorts of things.

Then they found something exceedingly interesting. The people at the anti end of the scale (I will drop the high and low now) were, for one thing, anti-everything. If they were women, they were anti-men, and if they were men, they were anti-women. If they were anti-labor, they were also anti-Negro, and if they were anti-Jews, they were also anti-Catholic. They were anti

V. Race Majority — Race Minority

whatever group they were not—not against any one in particular, but just plain *anti*.

It wasn't that they had special stereotypes about any particular group. They shared the stereotypes offered by society that had distinctions in them, but they worked them into a basic position that, if you analyzed it, was: "I can't bear for anybody in the world to be different from me. The world would be a very good place if everybody in it was my age, my sex, of my economic group, religion, race, and if their ancestors had immigrated at the same time. Then everybody would be just like me, and it would be quite tolerable."

So what you really found in those people was an inability to enjoy difference—any kind of difference, you see, even difference of sex.

Now, the typical anti-minority members—using *minority* in the sense of the group that is disapproved of or disallowed by the group that is talking—are people who cannot tolerate difference, who are threatened by it, who are frightened by it, who every time they have to face the fact that anybody in the world is different from themselves go into some sort of defensive opposition.

There is one other point I want to tell you about the people at the high anti end of the scale in this study: they appeared to be either excessively normal or psychotic—psychotic, not neurotic. That is, people who, if they cracked, would crack hard and would really break away from reality completely, who had a brittle relationship to the world, a relationship based upon so many falsifications that they had a continuous sense of living over a volcano, the thin crust of which they feared might break up. So that all their hostility toward other groups that might enter the same club or the same restaurant, any place where they were, was a frightened defense against fear: "What will happen if this is done to me? What will happen to me if I have to face one single more point of this kind?"

You can find this in the sort of man who leaves $125,000 to his club provided they will swear they will never let women in. That was done in one of our very famous intellectual clubs in this country. It is the sort of club that would normally, by this time, be fairly full of women. That will, you realize, meant that its maker had been safe in that club all his life, and he intended to hold on to that safety after death. He wasn't going to be invaded by women.

Well, that attitude toward letting minority groups eat in a restaurant where one eats, or join one's club, or anything of that sort, is a defense against invasion of a private world that cannot tolerate difference, cannot tolerate at all the fact that there are other people of another sort in the world.

At the other end of the scale, which is called the bottom, are the neurotics, the people who were actively pro-minority, pro minorities of which they were not members, of course. It is important to make the distinction. When I say pro-minority, I don't mean a Negro leader who is fighting for the position of Negro Americans. I do not mean Protestant leaders in Catholic communities, or Catholic leaders in Protestant communities, who are interested in looking after their own rights and defending their own people and giving them a better chance where they are. But by pro-minority, I mean the people who are minding other people's business, defending other people's minority positions.

V. Race Majority — Race Minority

I had a wonderful extreme example of this once when I was running a workshop. In the workshop was a leader who had been very much interested in all kinds of minorities. In this workshop three of our most blond, most privileged, most old-American girls thought they would like to have us put on some kind of drama that would show them what it was like to be a member of a minority group, so we said we would try it. The minute we started discussing it, this leader who had spent her life defending minorities got worried about those girls and wanted to defend them. For fifteen minutes they had been labeled a minority group, and she thought she ought to look after them. I thought they were doing very nicely without any help at all, but a mere definition put her on their side.

So the very extremely pro-minority group are people who have, you might say, built up into their personalities the discrepancies in our present society. In a sense that is what a neurotic is, someone who carries in his own body, in his own character, the fact that he has grown up in a society full of contradictions.

The people at the other, anti end of the scale won't recognize any contradictions. They may say things like "Labor is paid what it deserves," and "If the Negroes in America don't have any better education, it is because they don't have enough brains to take it; if they had, they'd take it and they'd have it." All the way through they justify the treatment of every minority group in terms of the fact that it gets exactly what it deserves. "There are no problems at all, and if everyone was just kept in his place, which is where he ought to be, which is a long way off from me, the world would be all right."

The neurotic who is very pro-minority, on the other hand, has been overexposed in his own experience to an understanding and a realization of the contradictions in our society. That usually means that he has had the personal experience of being an underdog in some fashion or other. He may have learned it by being a middle child in the family. You know the kind of family where there is one boy, and there are the eldest and the youngest daughters, and there is one other girl. Who is she? She's not the oldest, she's not the youngest, she's not the only boy. Who is she?

I heard one little girl of five say once: "When I die I'm going to leave everything to the next to the youngest." The emphasis that went into that at the age of five can develop into quite a lot of enthusiastic championing of the position of the underdog later. So that it is not surprising that one finds among these champions people who say that everything wrong is the fault of the majority.

You also get a considerable amount of exaggeration in this pro-minority group who blame the majority for anything. They say things like "There isn't any Jewish problem; it's not a Jewish problem, but a gentile problem," which one hears occasionally. And one hears also sometimes that "the problem of the Negro American is the problem of the white American," instead of being a problem for all concerned.

In the same way one could say also—I don't think it has ever been said, but there is no reason why not— "The problem of women is men's problem." I wonder how many of the men who agree with the other two points would like that, that women are just men's problem; that men created them, and if they are

V   Race Majority — Race Minority

troublesome to men, that is men's fault; men ought to bring them up better. Which is the end of the statement that says that any problem is the problem of the majority. The problem of two groups, actually—the equilibrium between the two groups, and the way the two groups face it—is a problem for everyone.

This is, of course, not true in a totalitarian country that has decided to kill all the members of a race, an intellectual group, or a religious group. There may be nothing whatever under those circumstances that a minority can do. In those circumstances members of such a minority have ceased to be interactive with the other people. They are like the witches in a New England community whom the community has decided to hang. From the moment a New England community decided to hang the witch, there wasn't much use in telling the witch she ought somehow to co-operate with the local preacher.

But leaving out those situations where an authoritative government has defined a group as non-human, the interaction between groups defined as part of a community is all groups' responsibility. Psychiatric problems are found at the other end of the scale, too, in the people who so over-champion every underdog that they interpret the rest of humanity not as mere mild overlords but as people who are spending their lives stepping on everybody else.

Then there are the sort of procedures in intergroup relations which start by arousing feelings of guilt. These are exceedingly common. A neurotic is usually an individual who feels pretty guilty about something. He feels he was treated badly by his family and probably in return has quite a few strong desires to do his family in. He represses these and has a certain amount of guilt about them, so his guilt makes him ready to atone, makes him care for other groups.

There is the speaker on race relations who does his level best to arouse the guilt feelings of an audience, as if each one of them had committed every sin against every minority group anywhere in the United States. In doing that the speaker is playing on neurotic tendencies of those in the audience.

I have never forgotten an experience of my own that illustrates quite well this particular implication of playing on guilt in the name of goodness. This happened when I was actively running a school in interracial relations, and I was sleeping, eating, and thinking nothing but intergroup relations. So I was professionally alert and should have been reasonably well-behaved—at least it would have been reasonable to expect me to behave better than most people on this score.

It happened on a university campus, and I had my four-year-old daughter with me. She was loitering along, and I wanted to get somewhere. I said to her: "Hurry."

And she said: "Oh, but I have got to eat some pine needles."

I said: "Oh, come on. Hurry up. You don't need to eat pine needles."

And she said: "I have to do it to get my vitamin C."

And I said: "But you're not an Indian. You don't have to get your vitamin C out of pine needles. You can get it out of oranges and grapefruit."

And she said: "*Why?* Why can't Indians get it out of oranges and grapefruit?"

And I said: "Because they're too poor to buy them."

V. Race Majority — Race Minority

And she said: "*Why* are they too poor to buy them?"

And then I made my fatal mistake. I said: "Because the white man took their lands away from them."

Then she made the first racial comment she had ever made. She stopped dead in her tracks and said: "Am I white?"

I said: "Yes, you are."

And she said: "But I didn't tooken their land away from them, and I don't like it to be tooken."

Superficially, that looks fine, and most of the people on the extreme pro-minority end of the California scale would say it was fine. "You have really implanted the right attitudes in that child. Now she'll be angry. She'll get angry at the way the white man treated the Indians and go on from that to be angry in the name of every minority."

But it wasn't a good thing. That indignation was the result of feeling herself identified as white and wicked. Up to that point she had only felt herself as a human being. I had no right to make that definition. The white man did not take the Indians' land. There is no such thing as The White Man any more than there is such a thing as The Indian.

What I should have said was that the early settlers in the Indian country took the land away. She wouldn't have asked: "Am *I* an early settler?" She would have asked: "What *is* an early settler?" And we could have gone on and talked about the early settlers, and the story of how they got the land away from the Indians could have been told in such a way as to put over all the ethical points just as clearly, plus the fact that the early settlers were more or less following out a good many of the standards of their own day. They weren't completely ruthless to the poor people, either, so one doesn't have to hate the early settlers, but should try to work for a society in which later settlers don't behave in the same way.

That trap is the neurotic trap in the whole situation, in which there is a tendency to play on the indignation and use it. I was using the stereotype, you see, a stereotype I had picked up. I would not have made that mistake if I had been dealing with Negro-American problems, but I had not been paying much attention recently to the Indians. I had mentioned the fact that vitamin C came from pine needles, and how the Indians were undernourished and nutritionists had found they could eat pine needles. It was a nice story. But the story I had heard in my childhood about the exploitation of the Indian I had also kept ready in pickled form to pass on to others.

Any society that is working at improving interracial relations and interreligious and intergroup relations is dependent for its progress on individuals who object to the current position. They seem necessary. The majority of society would simply stay still if only the group that is disadvantaged fought for its own cause. We have to have, simultaneously, those in the privileged position question their own right to it, and those who want the privileged position fight for it, to get a new point to the total society.

In the same way it is necessary for men in the law school to want women to get in, as well as women wanting to get in, if you are going to have women in a law school with any sort of comfort. If men don't want them, they don't get in. And if only the men wanted

V. Race Majority — Race Minority [143

them and there were no women wanting to get in, the women wouldn't get in either.

The same position applies to every change in status between groups in a community that will bring us closer to our ideal of each person being evaluated as a human being—not in terms of group membership, but in terms of what he or she is himself or herself.

Progress will always be retarded by the people who are protecting their sanity by denying that there is anything wrong and by refusing to deal with differences of any sort. Progress will be helped by the people who are overstating what is wrong, overstating it not in terms that they may define inaccurately, but overstating it because they are putting into the fight their own private emotion (because they were second children, or because they didn't get a second pair of shoes when their brother did) and want to punish others for what mother or brother or teacher did a long time ago.

Whoever originally built up the idea that the white man took the Indians' land away from them was setting up another racial stereotype, was blaming another group unfairly and doing something just as classificatory as those who say all immigrants or all Protestants or all Catholics do one thing or another.

We have two sorts of problems here, and I assume there are two kinds of people involved. One is the sort who are practically concerned with interracial group relations and intergroup relations, and for them this sort of analysis is useful in watching the tone that the whole movement takes, the way guilt is used. I have found, for instance, that if you scold an audience for having prejudice, or if you even inveigh against prejudice, you raise in your audience or in your group an answering hostility. When there is hostility in your voice, back it comes from them. You can't even attack an evil like prejudice before people who never thought about their prejudices before, who got their prejudices from their family, who didn't know they were wrong, without making a large number of them feel abused and hurt and angry, and fight back. So that some knowledge of the personality structure of different people and the way they are fighting is necessary.

The most gifted minority leader is likely to be a person who is proud to be who he is. He has been given a plus point; he grew up, even though he came from a very disadvantaged group, being told: "Be proud of who you are, be proud of what you are; your people are going some place." Having been told that—not that he should mind not being of some other race or of some other religion—he bears within him an impetus forward that makes it possible for him to carry along with him other members of his race, sect, group, or class who themselves glow with a much more flickering flame.

And the positive leader of a majority group is also a person who has been made proud of being himself, who has not been taught: "You are not, not, not, not something," but has been made proud of being the person he is.

At every point you have to watch for those who have been given strength by plus positions, and those who have been given various sorts of special slants by a negative position.

Our most fertile field for improving majority-minority relations is in our guidance of children. If you can

V. Race Majority — Race Minority

bring up your children to be glad they are of the sex they are and the age they are—that year—and to be glad of their religious ancestry, their racial ancestry, their national ancestry, and see that pride is not denied at any point by the fact that they are not something else, you are guaranteeing them the sort of character structure that will help them make their contribution in turn to working toward a world where no individual is ever negatively defined by any group membership that he cannot himself help.

1. Does our culture make excessive demands on the ego to be mature politically, professionally, and so on?

No, I would say that, on the other hand, our culture makes rather excessive demands on our being immature a very long time. The most perfectly adjusted persons in our society, probably those who in a sense are plus-adjusted—the people who will make the great contributions—are still maturing when they die.

Eskimo children are nicely matured at seven. They have to wait a little while before getting married, but everything else is there. They know every point completely and know how to handle every value in their society. They don't question anything. They wait until they are old enough to marry, and that's that.

Our society demands a degree of withholding of final judgments, of flexibility. It demands an unduly long adolescence, for one thing. It demands being able to change one's mind at thirty, forty, fifty, or sixty. I should say that is one of the great demands on people: to postpone final judgment, to remain flexible, not to become rigid, but be able to move and respond to the society and not settle down to any one position from which they are unable to change.

Our culture does make a strong demand on the ego in that we have to be able to choose. We are asked to have an ego that can choose, that does not have everything charted out for it. Our culture depends on an ego that must choose between right and wrong at every turn, because the right and the wrong are no longer sharply defined in so many different groups, and there are so many different standards. So if our culture is to survive and be comfortable, it has to be a fairly strong ego.

2. Do the children of mixed marriages—one parent of the majority group and one parent of a minority group —usually grow into more tolerant adults?

That is a nice question, because such a situation comes right on the razor's edge. It can be the breeding-ground of great tolerance. The child can grow up to belong to both groups, to be proud of both groups, to identify things in itself that it likes with each group.

Some American Indians tend to say, for instance, that in every mixed marriage there are a lot of children who are just mixed, but you get one Indian and one white, and they tend to push individual children toward the one position or the other as the child is told it acts like an Indian or like a white. If this is told by the opposite parent, it may be told in a friendly or an unfriendly fashion. It may be told positively or negatively.

V. Race Majority — Race Minority

There is quite a good anecdote [3] that is told of a group of Negro children in the South who were picking on one sibling who was much lighter than the others. The mother comes out (this is the sort of story that was told to deprecate certain relationships)—the mother comes out and says: "You chillun stop apickin' on dat pore white chile. He'd be jes' as black as you are if I hadn't got behind in mah insurance."

That story is a Negro-American joke which denies the fact that white people are the least interesting or attractive except for economic reasons. It is a counter-racial joke. But a mixed marriage may operate to make a child believe that it lives nowhere, that it is nobody, that it is just a mongrel. Or parents can use a mixed marriage to point out, every time the child does something, that it is like the race of the other parent, which is disparaged; and that has terrifically negative effects.

So that in one single situation you have the possibility of the whole gamut, depending primarily upon how the parents and siblings and neighbors handle the situation.

3. What do you think of genealogy as a hobby? Is it wrong to be proud of ancestors—the "Mayflower," 1066, and all that? Or is it neurotic?

I have already provided somebody in the audience with another group category to label somebody with—in this case "normal" and "neurotic." I

---

[3] A free rendering from memory of a story recorded on p. 168 of John Dollard's *Caste and Clan in a Southern Town* (New Haven: Yale University Press; 1937).

take it this questioner does not approve of this ancestor business. Wouldn't you think so? And now anybody at all who was interested in ancestors might run the risk of getting classified as a neurotic. You see how the thing works? You get rid of one set of categories and you probably create another.

I think it is fine to be interested in ancestors as long as the point of being interested in them isn't that they are better than other people. Ancestors are a lot of fun, and it is a great pity that because people have changed their country and their way of living so much in this country, so many American children are robbed of a picture of their past. But the child whose grandparents were Polish peasants or Italian peasants is robbed of the picture of his past just because of the behavior of some of the people who claim descent from immigrants in the *Mayflower*. We have got to have a little better method of looking at these things.

4. Please define the excessively normal people you spoke of. What are they like?

You know, they are just awfully good fellows, people who have completely expected reactions to everything, who would never make any sort of awkwardness, the sort of people whose manners are just what you would expect them to be. That means they are as rude and disapproving as possible of the groups that they are expected to be rude to and disapproving of.

Their hair is awfully well done, they are the sort of people you can rely on. You know they'll never make a scene anywhere, and they are just *so* careful of public

V. Race Majority — Race Minority

opinion. Some people think of them that way, and others classify them as excessively normal. They fit the ads a little too well.

5. As an anthropologist, what is your explanation of the Irish question?

I should say one of the points about the Irish question is that the Irish immigrants to America were able to overestimate their position in passing it on to their children. That is certainly so in those areas where they do not become Americans although they stay here, but where unto the third and fourth generation they describe themselves as Irish.

That might be described as the sort of plus that the Brahmins have, you know, a transmutation of too many ancestors into kings. That can be a little dangerous. That is the Irish question as it is seen in America.

The Irish question as it is seen in the Old World was a part of the whole move toward nationalism, and of the desire of each people for their own freedom and for their own political institutions, which went with their own way of life. And in a sense the Irish were as helpless as any other group that has been caught in the desire for national independence. That desire has swept the world, and as far as we can see is going on sweeping parts of Asia.

Nationalism is an invention. Once it has been invented, any people who love their country are helpless against it. And the Irish, of course, love their country enormously. You only need to read Irish poetry and all the poetry about Ireland—"My Dark Rosaleen," for instance—to realize they are a people who have a great affection for their own country.

The Poles are another group who have enormous affection for their country, for their nationality, and are especially susceptible to an invention like nationalism, which says that any country that is not free is downtrodden, is defiled, has been placed in a terrible position.

So you have people with a plus view of themselves, a plus view of their ancestors, a plus view of their country, who nevertheless are sometimes put in a position of fighting a terrific battle out of a plus position rather than a negative one.

6. In which direction can American democracy look for greater minority equality, educational, economic, or political?

Now, I think that that question is probably not usefully phrased. It is very often phrased that way. The author of *An American Dilemma*[4] makes a list of privileges the Negro American wants that he does not have, and the privileges that the white American is most willing to give him. Then he shows how they meet. That is, the Negro American would say he wants economic equality most. The white American is most willing to give economic equality and privilege where he won't give the others, so the planning in free relations can, so he says, start here. Where that is true, that course is useful. But there are parts of this coun-

---

[4] Gunnar Myrdal: *An American Dilemma* (New York: Harper & Brothers; 1944).

V. *Race Majority — Race Minority* [151

try where economic competition is more important than other sorts, where it is easier to get people to go to church together than to go into a factory together.

I think the main principle is that we must take the point the minority group wants most, the point the majority group is most willing to concede, and work on that first, and continue from there.

7. **How can we get women themselves to be satisfied with their bodies and with what they are?**

I should say you can't do a whole lot with the current generation. Those who have been brought up with the handicap are probably not going to be able to get over it.

We can do a good deal with the future generation through education. Girls are perfectly satisfied if they are not eternally told that boys can do things they can't do, and that "Your brother, well, after all, he needs a better education, because he's going to have to do this or that, and do something you can't do."

In order to make women satisfied to be themselves, you need two things: a social system in which girls can do the things they are gifted to do, which may be quite different from what men can do, and in which the careers that women follow are treated with dignity, and nobody says: "She's just keeping house," or "doing nothing," which is the other word for housekeeping. And you also need methods of bringing up children in the home that will support such a system.

8. What should be the group attitude toward homosexuals?

I think that is a good problem to bring up, because they are a minority group that crop up in almost every large society, and the question brings out one point I meant to talk about and did not get to. That is, the minority in any society are punished because they do something one has decided not to do oneself.

Now, almost all minorities are classified as inferior and are always endowed with all bad behavior. They tend to be regarded as more sexually potent than the majority group. They get drunk, they have a wonderful time, and the majority group is busy being respectable and controlling its impulses.

You get that not only in interracial and religious groups. You know the stories you can tell with a Yorkshire accent or a Cockney dialect that you couldn't tell in plain English. And almost every society has an accent in which you can tell disreputable stories. Everybody relaxes and says: "Oh, it's not about me. Isn't it fun?"

In our handling of any group in the population whose solutions of life are different from those of the majority, the majority's difficulty is their fear that they will follow the path of the minority.

A society that was not worried for fear most of its population won't be heterosexual most of the time would not have to persecute homosexuals.

V. *Race Majority — Race Minority* [153

9. How would you combat the statement used by anti people: "the majority rules"?

The majority rules within an ethical system. The majority rules within the Constitution, and within the guarantees of the Constitution. The majority does not rule without a framework. That is one of the things, I think, that are most commonly misunderstood.

The majority rules in relation to the code or standards of ethics of a total society, and within that code, within that Constitution, under the rulings of the Supreme Court the majority rules. But there is no known ethic that is merely the majority rule. I don't think any society has ever tried it.

It is very interesting that societies that have decided not to be so unethical as they really are, and to say: "We're a bad lot; let's face it, and let's standardize it and set it up," tend on the whole to be very autocratic societies and not societies that go in for majority rule.

10. How can one define difference if one cannot use other people as examples?

It is all right to define difference, provided you define both kinds of difference—good difference and bad difference—and provided that you do not associate the difference you are disapproving with a group.

For instance, if we want to have mixed racial education for children, one of the most important things we feel is that we don't want to have a class with only one child of one race in it and say twenty of another. The child of the minority race may be nice or may be very nasty, because there are both kinds of people in every race. Unless we are able to give our children examples of the fact that they can like or dislike or they can be neutral toward the individuals of the other group, they will tend to generalize from the one to the many.

So if you say: "I don't want you to throw snowballs through the window like that Bill. Yesterday I saw him throw a stone through the window in the butcher shop. He hit the butcher in the eye and broke his glasses. That's not the kind of behavior I want in you"—when you say it, don't call him "that horrid little Protestant," or "that little Polack," or "that little Center Street gangster," or "that little street child." Call him Bill, the boy who threw the snowball through the window.

11. How can we ever be too pro-minority group with the state of attitudes and behavior against such groups being as hostile and unfair as it is?

That is just the point I made, that if you define an all-out position on behavior in some other group than your own, it is usually in terms of an attack, a definition of the other group as hostile and unfair.

Most people in the United States are not hostile to whatever group they do not belong to. They are lazy, indifferent, stereotyped members of their own society. They do not have the time to be hostile, and very often have not even met the groups they talk about.

They live in a society that has inherently a very large number of bad arrangements, many of which came out

V. Race Majority — Race Minority

of the historical conditions under which different groups came to this country. One group came from an educated group or class, another came from a peasant group, and they brought with them the attitudes of that group which went with the class system. These people today are the inheritors of those attitudes. To call them hostile and unfair I don't think does any good.

We want to change the conditions that exist in this country, but if we label as "hostile" the position of those who are the unwitting and often thoughtless continuers of something they have inherited, I think we undo much of what we should like to do.

12. **How does the interpretation of discrimination as shown by a person who (perhaps subconsciously) feels himself in or as a minority fit into your theory?**

If the individual who interprets or feels himself as a minority does so without hostility, then he is the perfect interpreter, because he understands. Most of our great religious leaders, after all, who have espoused the cause of the hungry and the poor and the needy, probably had a chance to touch more perfectly than most people upon what it means to be hungry and poor and needy in some other sense. But they are great religious leaders because they could do that positively, without attacking, without building up so much hostility that they were not able to gather people around them.

13. Do you advise parents to tell children to be proud of what they are? Isn't pride about what was, after all, an accident of birth rather foolish?

I am glad somebody brought that point up. I evidently didn't state it very well. You have to teach a child to be proud—to be really proud, in this sense of the word—only of those things that they do themselves, only of those things for which they are responsible. I mean, if you paint a good picture or make a good cake, or run a good race, then you can be proud. And I shouldn't really have used the word *proud*; I might have used the word *glad* much more aptly. I think we do owe it, if possible, to children to give them a sense of gladness in those things which surely are an accident of birth and for which they are not responsible. Nevertheless, everyone who carries his own culture with him and really gives it to the next generation has the possibility of giving it with gladness, of communicating to a child the positive things about being Irish or being a New Englander. You can make it more agreeable, you can make it all plus. Baked beans can be something you eat because it is thrifty and frugal, or baked beans can be what we have on Saturday night because Grandma came from New England.

14. Why reinforce the differences? Why not work for a positive approach to one world, one religion, being like others?

A great deal of the motive force for democracy, for equality, for the rights of the minority groups,

V. Race Majority — Race Minority

comes from the position that we are all children of God and we are all human beings on earth. That has been a great missionary force in the world.

But if you do that alone, you lose the chance to cultivate all the values that different societies have built up, to cultivate the beauty of the different races, of every race. Instead you move to the problem of those who get their hair either dekinked or permanently waved, so they will look as much alike as possible. You deprecate physical differences, you deprecate intellectual differences, you deprecate artistic gifts, you deprecate the contribution that each religion has made, you deprecate the beauty of different languages, the beauty of different cultures.

And although we have to have an over-all framework—that we are all human beings, that we do live in One World—the refusal to recognize differences is a short cut to what looks like equality and democracy, but what in most cases where it is put into effect means a compulsory attempt to make everyone like something he is not.

VI

STUDENT — TEACHER

by CLYDE KLUCKHOHN, PH.D.[1]

BECAUSE as we discuss any human relationship we need to have a common basis of understanding, I want first of all to say something about my own conception of mental health. Anthropological research has greatly widened and deepened the psychiatrist's conception of the normal. We now know that some types of personality fail to find fulfillment in one way of life, or culture, as the anthropologist calls it, whereas there is reason to suppose that these types might have flourished in another.

Some cultures allow latitude for a wide range of personal adjustments; in others, the individual who does not conform to the single pattern is punished so severely that he becomes neurotic, or perhaps, if there is a constitutional predisposition, he becomes psychotic.

Behavior regarded as abnormal in one society is acceptable in another. As a matter of fact, not so very long ago all standards for normality seemed on the point of disappearing in the face of a kind of complete relativism. It was said, to caricature a bit: "Well, if the Bugabuga can do it and they seem to think it is all right, what is wrong with my doing it?"

Today, however, it is agreed that certain sorts of

[1] Harvard. Professor of Anthropology, Harvard University; past president of the American Anthropological Association.

VI. Student — Teacher

mental reaction are considered abnormal in every society. It is also possible to have universal standards of normality not merely because some standards are found in all ways of life, but also because of the information a set of symptoms gives as to the functioning of the personality as a whole. In any culture certain symptoms indicate malfunctioning. Note: it isn't just a set of symptoms; it is a set of symptoms as it plays a role in the economy of the personality. You cannot, however, simply read off a list of items of behavior and say: "Anybody who behaves that way is abnormal in any society. Period."

The conception that aggression and hostility are neurotic or maladaptive, and are the symptoms of an adult who has been chronically frustrated in infancy and childhood, is a culture-bound view of our middle-class psychiatrists. In our own society, in lower-class families physical aggression of some types is as normal, in the sense of socially approved behavior, as it is in frontier communities the world over. So we must always question whether outward indications of aggression and hostility are, in their cultural context, merely habits of escape from reality that temporarily lessen anxiety but that do not relieve it at its root source.

It is necessary, in my opinion, in making a definition of mental health, to take three things into consideration: first, what has often been called adaptation. That is, does the individual behave in such a way that he survives? An individual who jumps in front of trains is not very likely to survive, so this is one kind of behavior which, under almost all circumstances, in all societies, is abnormal.

Second, there is the conception of adjustment. That

is, does an individual behave in such a way that he gets along, that he not only survives physically but finds life tolerable, that he makes enough peace with the demands of his society, that he gets enough pleasure out of life to be motivated to keep going?

I think in recent American psychiatry there has probably been an overemphasis upon adaptation and adjustment, and not enough emphasis upon internal integration or harmony; that is, upon developing the type of personality in which the means and the ends that an individual has adopted are harmonious, and in which the means are adequate to attain the ends. This is my third consideration.

Now, we can have individuals who are adjusted and adapted—we all know many of them, people who stay out of jail and out of the insane asylum—and yet whose lives by their own testimony are empty. They feel their lives are incoherent; they do not feel perfection in even some moments of their existence. It is only when one brings these various criteria together, I think, that one finds the ideal type of mental health. One then finds the person who identifies cordially and from inside with both the conserving and the innovating forces of his society. This person expresses the full value of his capacities, and by virtue of this complete expression also presents a full or complete value to society. Student-teacher relationships promoting such mental health are what we are interested in.

Before going further into the student-teacher relationship, it is also necessary to establish a little context in our culture, because you cannot talk about the student-teacher relationship in the abstract; you must talk about it as culturally defined.

VI. Student — Teacher

Our American theory of education insists, explicitly or implicitly, that both the emotional and the intellectual aspects of individual development are involved. This is in contrast to certain other theories in the rest of the Western World. Take the French notion, at least at the level of higher education. It tends to be an almost purely intellectual one; for instance, French professors, even at the *lycée* level, are not expected to participate in a community of learning with their students. They are there to give the student facts and scientific theories.

It rather reminds me of Maurois's book on English character, *The Silence of Colonel Bramble*.[2] In it the French liaison officer with the British Army in the First World War remarks to his English colleagues that he is astonished at how little Oxford graduates know about Debussy and Proust. The British officer to whom he is talking replies that he has a false conception of the educational process as the English think about it, that the end of the English educational system is not to fill people's heads with a lot of culture with a capital C, but to impregnate people with the point of view of their class in society, without which they would be dangerous to themselves and to their class.

Our system, I think, is somewhere between those two, perhaps a combination of them. If you get professors talking, you could document the French notion. Hyper-intellectualism is, of course, an occupational disease of college professors. In a document called *General Education in a Free Society*, produced

[2] André Maurois: *The Silence of Colonel Bramble* (New York: D. Appleton & Co.; 1930).

by some of my colleagues at Harvard four or five years ago, it is unhappily a fact that about two hundred pages are given to the disembodied framework of the pure intellect, so to speak, and about six pages to the human side. Nevertheless we have tended to regard the American educational system, as a whole, not only as a means for acquiring the three R's and other skills, but as a way of transmitting our traditional American values, as a way of teaching discrimination in appreciation of various things—in enjoyment, in sympathy, and so on.

If you look at our public-school system, it is clear that our formal educational program now has, implicitly or explicitly, some of the functions that used to be those of the family, and some of those that used to be reserved to the Church. This is one of the reasons that we make life so difficult for teachers in our public schools. It is why we hedge them about with all kinds of restrictions that we would usually consider undemocratic. Outstanding examples of this are prevalent in most small towns: the public-school teacher, if she smokes, must smoke in private; and no matter how she may feel privately about religion, she must be seen with a reasonable regularity in the pew of some church on Sunday.

This is because, I think, we do feel not only that our teachers are transmitters of knowledge and of skills, but that they are also custodians and transmitters of our moral values, and that therefore they have to be acceptable. They have to be models of the predominantly middle-class code of our society.

I think that this sharing of family functions is symbolized in other ways. In the elementary school the

VI. Student — Teacher

teacher, who is still ordinarily a woman, is quite frankly regarded as a mother surrogate, as a substitute for the mother. In the usual junior-high-school system today, the children go into different classrooms in groups divided according to the subject matter to be recited at that particular hour. But each pupil also has a "home room" with a "home-room teacher." This "home" terminology suggests at least an unconscious intention to carry on the close connection between the institution of teaching and the institution of the home.

I think that it is perhaps also significant that in this home room are applied the same criteria as in the family. In theory, and to a considerable extent in practice, parents are very careful to avoid favoritism between children and to try their best to treat one child on exactly the same level as another. So in the home room, in contrast to all other school groupings, an effort is made to assign people alphabetically, or by some strictly objective system, rather than by ability or by other evaluations.

Now, keeping in mind that in our culture teachers are regarded as in part parents or close to parents, almost as the priests or medicine men are in a primitive society, let us look at the primarily personal dimension of the student-teacher relationship. I am going to speak later about the primarily social or socio-cultural dimension. You cannot really separate the two, but it is convenient to make a distinction regarding the primary emphasis.

Students and teachers both come to their relationship with already formed emotional needs and emotional patterns of a particular sort, and they both recognize or want to feel—certainly the students want to feel—that this relationship has a personal as well as an official quality.

One sees this not only in the primary grades but even at the most advanced level of university teaching. I remember a few years ago a large seminar of graduate students at which four or five of the senior members of a particular university department spoke. The first four spoke well, not only in my judgment, but in terms of the students' own judgment; but they spoke coldly. They laid the facts on the line, but they laid them down without even icy enthusiasm.

The fifth man, who was frankly regarded as somewhere between a charlatan and a fool by both his colleagues and a majority of the graduate students, made an appeal to the will as well as to the head. He talked what, if you looked at it cold-bloodedly on paper, 99.44 per cent of people in the room would have agreed was arrant nonsense and intellectual demagoguery. But when he finished, the ninety graduate students in the room burst out in spontaneous applause, because what he gave them was what the four previous speakers had not. It points up that the whole student-teacher relationship has an emotional personal aspect, or at least a desired emotional and personal content, and it has to be seen reciprocally in those terms.

One of the difficulties, of course, particularly in our contemporary mass production of education both in the universities and in the schools, is that whatever you do you can't satisfy all of the customers either intellectually or emotionally. You just can't. They are too diverse.

This may seem to be a counsel of despair, but I don't

VI. *Student — Teacher*

think it is. I think a recognition of this fact is essential to the development of a healthy relationship between teacher and pupil. The differences—just sheer constitutional differences—that all of us have permit me as a teacher to speak meaningfully in whole-person terms to a few of a class, I hope; but to some of them I can only speak meaningfully, in varying degrees, to a lesser extent; and inevitably (and I don't feel defeated by this) I am going to leave some of them cold, and annoy some of the rest of them. That is just in the nature of the case.

I think we have to be most skeptical of any formula that says: "This is the way, machinelike, to teach, to establish a healthy relationship between teacher and student." It is, by premise, false and misleading.

Some of our earlier conceptions of education ("spare the rod and spoil the child," and so on) tended to repress one type of personality expression which is natural, perhaps all too natural, to some of us. But the so-called progressive education movement was equally repressive to another group, whom Sheldon and the constitutional anthropologists call "cerebrotonics"; lean, æsthetic people with lots of brain, lots of skin surface, and somewhat (in ordinary language) introverted. To say: "Now, the natural, normal thing for everybody to do is to mix in, to get socialized, to take part in group activities," is just as hard on people with this innate bent as the older style of education was on a certain different minority, the expansive extroverts.

So it seems to me that the first principle is that of recognition of diversity, recognition of different needs. One has to deal with some kinds of students in one way, in a way that with them may be very successful but will be equally unsuccessful if you apply it as a mechanical formula to another sort of person with a different temperamental bent.

Always, I think, we run the danger, in religion and in educational systems, of using a way of doing things which has its merits, has its great merits for some people, but which satisfies twenty or sixty or seventy per cent only to some degree and fails to bring out and develop more than a few tenths of the potentialities that are in human beings.

The second point I should like to make on handling the student-teacher relationship is the tremendous need for self-understanding on the part of teachers, since more can be expected of us than we have a right to expect of immature children or youngsters. We have to ask ourselves some very honest questions: what are our personal motives in teaching or doing a particular kind of teaching? And if we are honest and also rational, we shall realize that there is almost never a perfect fit between the official goals of the educational system in which we are operating, and which intellectually we may fully accept, and our private and personal motives.

If a woman, by her own choice or through the accidents of fortune, is a spinster and is likely to remain one, she will do well to recognize the role that teaching plays as a substitute for motherhood in the economy of her personality. There is nothing in this to be ashamed of. The only important thing is to realize it and to realize its implications, for only then is it possible intelligently to capitalize the good side of it and to avoid the bad.

In a society like ours, where, as we all know, the

VI. Student — Teacher

greatest prestige rewards and economic rewards do not go to teachers, there are some tough questions about motives that we have to ask ourselves. There is always the possibility that you or I have gone into teaching as a kind of escape from a sterner sort of competition, as a way perhaps of achieving cheap and easy dominance that we could not have attained so easily in a large corporation or a law office. Motives, of course, are never simple; they are all mixed. Frequently in teaching there is the motive, usually unconscious, of getting hold of a group of people who cannot talk back to you. But such self-interest may to some extent be mixed with genuinely and deeply idealistic motives.

To the extent that one gains some self-insight into these matters, one is less likely to project—that is, to treat one's pupils as objects of an aggression that really is based upon one's relations with other people. Insight makes it a bit easier to resist taking out on one's class the kind of hostility and antagonism that is perhaps engendered in the home situation.

Students, especially the older ones, can also get some self-knowledge here—and I think teachers can help them get this. A high-school youngster or a college girl or boy may be reacting toward a teacher not as to an individual person with certain qualities, but as to a father or a mother, as to a figure of authority toward whom some antagonism is felt. A teacher may recognize this and help the young person to realize it. To the extent that both teacher and student realize the deeper motivations in the relationship as well as the official motivations, there will be greater health in this particular human relationship.

It seems to me that the role of the teacher is somewhat between that of the psychiatrist and that of the parent. It is a kind of mixture of the personal and the impersonal. That is, the teacher is not, and in my opinion should not be, unlike the psychoanalyst, a kind of blank screen on which the patient projects his difficulties; nor, on the other hand, can he expect to have the kind of relationship that a close relative can have, because pupils and teachers both move through time.

Practically all students have problems. In a recent survey of a group of so-called normal college students selected on the basis of satisfactory academic records, no evidence of disciplinary problems from the dean's office, no evidence of psychiatric troubles from the hygiene department, and other criteria for their normality, almost all were found on close study to have problems of a somewhat troubling nature. In fact, ninety per cent were shown to have such problems.

So this relationship between teacher and student has an emotional dimension that must be considered with the same rationality as more mechanical problems such as the effect upon learning of opening and shutting windows and getting light in the students' eyes, and all similar things taught in certain courses in certain teachers' colleges.

There are some other things that could and perhaps should be said here, but, once again, so much depends upon the nature of the situation. An individual person-to-person relation, a small class, a large class, and other similar variables present different relationship situations. There are only a few very general things that it seems to me possible to say.

One is that in a large class, for instance, one wants to steer a middle ground between two types of teach-

VI. Student — Teacher

ers. There is the type who sedulously avoids any kind of rapport with his or her class, who refuses to look at the class and walks up and down and away and seems to be putting a kind of taboo down and saying: "Don't touch me. Don't come near me. I am here to give you some facts. Period." And there is the other type of teacher who on the platform before a large class appears to be giving his all personally as well as intellectually, and who rouses in the students a kind of anticipation of close personal relationship that in reality he can never hope to fulfill, and who therefore makes them feel cheated and resentful.

I think one has to strike a middle course between giving the students the kind of emotional support they want and need and allowing them to be too submissive, to be too dependent.

Finally, we must guard against a mistake that I believe many of us make. I think we have to be very careful, particularly in early relations with a certain group of students, not to overwhelm them, either in the number of facts that we throw at them or with too much warmth all at once. Particularly in adolescence, but to some extent in younger children also, there is a great fear of being overwhelmed.

Now I should like to turn for a few minutes to what I would call the primarily social dimension. Here you have the whole problem of the teacher's place in the larger community, and the teacher's relationships specifically to parents, to the school board, and to other parts of the community.

Here I think our culture, our way of life, is at fault. The main job to be done here is a problem not only for teachers, who have a hard enough time as it is to adjust to the situation as currently defined for them; it is a problem for society as a whole.

The one thing that I have time to develop on these broad social aspects of teacher-student relationships is the problem of social class. It is part of our traditional ideology to say that we have no social classes in America; and indeed there is a certain important sense in which we are, alone among large countries, a middle-class culture. We do not, I think, have social class in the sense in which certain of the older European countries have it, or at any rate have had it. But I think that the work of William Lloyd Warner [3] and John Dollard and other social anthropologists has shown us—whether we like it or not—that within a particular time period, in a particular community, there are varying groups of social intimacy. Only to a limited extent do people—parents and children—move freely from one to another such group except in a few comparatively peripheral and comparatively formalized cross-class organizations such as the American Legion, church groups (to some extent), and the Y.M.C.A. and Y.W.C.A. If you examine who visits whom, who talks to whom, who lets my children play with her children, and the like, you will find in most American communities today that fairly sharp forms of class structure, forms that are considerably sharper than our traditional beliefs would permit, have crystallized.

These dividing lines are closely connected with occupational and economic position, but they are not

[3] W. Lloyd Warner, Marcia Meeken, and Kenneth Eells: *Social Class in America* (Chicago: Science Research Associates; 1949).

VI. Student — Teacher

identical with it, because to some extent the groups that have the highest position in the social class hierarchy are not the richest groups.

I do not think we need necessarily accept for the country as a whole the Warner divisions of upper, upper-lower, lower-lower, and so on. These may work in some communities; I am sure that they do not in others. But taking the country as a whole, and taking a generation as a time unit, I think there are in almost all communities some fairly stabilized social-intimacy groups that tend to have their own particular value systems, their own particular motivational system, their own habits, definitions of life, and conceptions of their goals. This has very important implications for the teacher-pupil relationship, because if you will take all of the teachers in your elementary schools, at least ninety-five per cent are in some sense middle-class.

They may not have been born as middle-class people. Some of them, through their own efforts and the sacrifices of their parents, have moved up to middle-class position. This mobility makes them all the more tenacious of middle-class values. Now, while ninety-five per cent of elementary-school teachers are middle-class, of their pupils more than one half, in economic terms and also in the more limited sense of social class, are lower-class. And nearly one third are what Warner calls "lower-lower"—slum culture, if you like.

These two groups have very different pictures of the situation in which they are involved. The meaning of learning and of certain specific things such as cleanliness, promptness, and achievement has one significance to the teacher in terms of her middle-class value system, and a different one for her lower-class pupils.

So that the two—and it goes both ways—tend to misinterpret each other's behavior. Social class limits and patterns the whole learning environment.

In a society like ours where, as somebody has said, everybody is all the time either going up or going down and is worried about it, there is obsessive emphasis upon the achievement principle, and a kind of naïve trust in such things as intelligence tests. This is particularly true of middle-class people, and most particularly of those who have themselves only recently won middle-class status.

If you talk to a teacher who genuinely thinks she is doing a perfectly honest job, fair to all, and point out certain discriminations, she says: "Well, but there's a difference in ability between those I have put in Group A and those I have put in Group B." Yet when you ask how ability was determined, you find out that it was determined by so-called intelligence tests.

Now, there is no such thing as a culture-free intelligence test, and the intelligence tests that we use in our schools are based precisely upon factors (a) which are most highly valued by the middle class, and (b) which middle-class children from birth on have the best opportunity of learning. To a considerable extent intelligence tests are simply a way of sorting people according to their socio-economic and class background.

It is a vicious circle, a very vicious circle. It tends to result in teachers punishing—I do not mean physically but psychologically punishing—lower-class children for having certain habits with regard to cleanliness and other things that come inevitably out of their background and that have nothing whatsoever to do

VI. Student — Teacher

with their innate intelligence or other innate capacity. They are punishing them psychologically as if these children had full access to all the norms and values of the middle class and then willfully—one might almost add sinfully—rejected them.

You do not promote social mobility in that way, and since slum pupils have little opportunity to learn the teacher's culture in any but a purely formalistic sense, teachers must do something to familiarize themselves with the cultural environment and the cultural motivation of their slum pupils. That does not mean accepting, but it does mean knowing, and knowing in emotional terms.

Unless and until teachers learn their pupils' cultural beliefs, their cultural definitions of life's problems, the special meaning of their words rather than the dictionary meanings, their culturally learned conceptions of the teacher and of the school; until teachers learn what their words mean to pupils from a different social class; until they know fully what pupils have to unlearn and what learning experiences are pleasant or painful—until then the net result of much teaching in the American public schools will be simply to depress, to lower the motivation of the underprivileged classes to learn.

Finally, if schools, our schools, are to be real agencies for mental health, the economic and social place of the teacher in the community must be improved. This is particularly true of teachers in our public-school systems. Lest I be thought of as on the defensive and injured here myself, I may say that I think professors at Harvard are, on the whole, well treated in these terms probably far better than we deserve. But in the

American public-school system by and large, the status of the teacher in the total community is doubtful. It is hedged about with all sorts of unnatural restrictions; it is underpaid and underprivileged. And in our educational system as well as elsewhere, bitter, frustrated people breed bitterness and frustration.

There is a need in the school system for selection of new teachers in some terms of mental health, just as much as there is in a profession like medicine, and increasingly in the Christian ministry and priesthood. There is need also for help for those who are in the system at present. That help, of course, should be put on the same basis as going to see a dentist. I don't mean—don't misunderstand me—that we should all, so to speak, psychoanalyze one another, that we should be like that fabled island where everybody lived by taking in everybody else's washing. It does not need to go to extremes at all. But I do think that there is need for a greater degree of self-insight, a greater knowledge of the principles of mental health, a greater knowledge of principles of group dynamics generally in our whole educational system, and not least in the colleges.

If this were achieved, there is real hope that teachers could pass on as a kind of by-product in their teaching what psychiatry and social science have learned about human behavior in general, just as physicians in the favorable case pass on to the population at large a knowledge of public health which makes for the greater good of the total society.

In conclusion, I should just like to mention once again the need for an awareness of the problems of social class and for a consequent avoidance of methods

VI. Student — Teacher

of teaching and of appraising through class-bound intelligence tests that depress the motivation of underprivileged groups, because our American way of life is deeply committed—and up to this point history has justified us in the commitment—to the belief that the potentialities of ability and creativity are not bounded by the particular socio-economic group in which an individual is born. Our society has been, until recently, a very fluid society and I think that it will augment the soundness of the student-teacher relationship in the deepest sense if this fluidity is continued.

It is terribly difficult to deal with some of these problems, and, curiously enough, most difficult within the academic profession, which ought to be the most rational; but academic culture is one of the most conservative and ritualized aspects of human behavior. Its formalization, its lack of functional connection with the daily problems of life, have given us a fossilized, bloodless character.

Just the sheer fact that for over a generation no basically new types of mental problems have been added to intelligence tests shows how fossilized some aspects of our system are. Here and elsewhere we have to deepen our self-awareness, our insight into ourselves as individuals and as members of a wider community and of a culture. Only to the degree that we do this can we dynamically and constructively handle student-teacher relationships.

1. What relation does a so-called intelligence test have with children's clean hands? A child's reaction to the test is what produces the result of the test, not whether

a child's hands are clean or not. Please make your point clearer.

I think that I am legitimately being ticked off. I mentioned cleanliness because it is one of the things that are most often brought up by teachers in justifying discrimination between one group of students and another.

But in addition to this there are also, in terms of vocabulary, very considerable class differences. That is, every child comes to school with a certain vocabulary that the child has acquired in the home and from the parents' friends and from children of the parents' friends. And while the child is in school, that vocabulary is added to, out of school as well as in school.

A study by Havighurst and Davis, of the School of Education of the University of Chicago, has shown very conclusively, for my money, that the vocabulary used in certain intelligence tests places undue weighting upon certain words that a middle-class child has an excellent opportunity to learn and picks up naturally from his environment. He acquires these words not because he has greater intelligence but because he has a better opportunity to acquire them.

So far as the nonverbal intelligence tests are concerned, many of them are also prejudiced in favor of types of learning about gadgets and other sorts of things easily picked up by a child who lives in a middle-class home, where there are refrigerators, radios, and various other electric and gas appliances. He has certain knowledge about how these things work that a child from a lower-level home does not have.

Once again, it does not require any intelligence in

VI. *Student — Teacher*

the sense of native capacity to solve many problems; it requires only the capacity to learn certain answers that other people have worked out.

For instance, I come into a room and turn the lights on. Well, the intelligence behind the lights is very considerable, but it does not require any intelligence in the problem-solving sense on my part to learn how to turn the lights on. That is a very simple thing that I learn out of my environment, a solution somebody else has given me.

It is these solutions learned by class membership that the studies of Davis, Havighurst, and others have shown to be weighted in favor of children who have lived at a high socio-economic level.

2. Why do some people ridicule the schoolmarm instead of respecting her as a community leader? Is it an unconscious jealousy or resentment of authority, or is it a desire to punish the single woman?

That is a very thoughtful question, and I think there is probably something to each of the points that have been suggested there.

I think in a society like ours today, where an increasing number of women are prepared for a profession but are not in fact allowed to have one, or are allowed to have it only at the price of not being married, or if married at the price of not having a family, probably there is a certain amount of unconscious, and maybe occasionally even semiconscious jealousy on the part of the woman who is tied down by a household, with no servants and two or three small children. From where she sits the teacher who has to be on duty only from eight in the morning until four in the afternoon, who has two weeks at Christmas and one week at Easter and three months in the summer, does have it easy. And not only does she have it easy; it goes much deeper than that. From the point of view of the tied-down married woman, the teacher also has an opportunity to practice and use some of the things that she learned in college and to have a kind of continuity in her life.

Many housewives, I think, feel: "Well, it was certainly nice majoring in Greek and Latin for four years, but where did it lead to? There is no thread between that part of my life and this part of my life."

I think, incidentally, that one of the things that our society needs to straighten out is the discrimination against married women teachers and teachers with children. I don't think for a minute that one has to be married to be a good teacher or to have children to be a good teacher, any more than I think one has to be psychoanalyzed. But other things being at all equal, and speaking statistically and only statistically, the betting odds are that a woman who has had a "normal" family life has a better chance of avoiding some of the emotional pitfalls—particularly the unconscious ones—in relations with her students.

There are obviously many different dimensions to this question. Given the rule that a woman teacher cannot be married or, at any rate, cannot be married and have children and continue to teach, one of the most troublesome dimensions is the extent to which teaching is stereotyped by the public as just a kind of stepping-stone for women.

VI. Student — Teacher

There has grown up this very vicious and false stereotype that a woman goes into teaching as a stepping-stone to getting married and going out into normal life; or if she remains a teacher, she is the spinster type. Obviously this is not a factual picture; I repeat that it is a stereotype. And I think that this is one of the reasons—a bad one, but at the emotional level a real one—for some of the attitudes.

There is also, I think, an unfortunate attitude toward men teachers—another stereotype. To teach permanently, at any rate in an elementary school, unless he is either a principal or an administrator or a coach, means, in this stereotype, that there is something inherently unmanly about the individual. "Well, here is this weakling who couldn't get out and be a go-getter in the hurly-burly of American men, and therefore, unless he is an administrator or a coach, there is something a little suspicious about him." The whole thing is of a piece with our overweening worship of the bitch goddess Success—success defined in narrow terms. Anybody who does not go in for cutthroat competition in certain narrowly defined paths is subject to ridicule.

During the war, I, like a lot of other professors, was in Washington for a while. When I had to go and deal with a general or an admiral, the first and worst hurdle to get over—and I could not always get over it—was just the sheer occupational stigma of being a professor. Then of course in many minds that was squared by being a professor at Harvard! It is a very complicated problem, involved with the whole structure of our society and with our definition of values.

3. Could you state briefly what Warner means by social class, and what percentage of the population is in each major class?

Warner [4] defines social class in terms of certain empirical criteria. Some of them are things like this: who visits whom regularly, who has whom to her small parties, who has whom only to her big parties, who calls upon whom, the children of what families go to dancing parties together, are encouraged parentally to marry, and a great many other specific things of that kind.

Then another criterion is the plus judgments that people express when they talk about their own social relationships. They say: "He's one of us," or "She is one of us," "They're our kind"; or they say: "No, they are high-society folks," or "They put on airs," or "She snubbed me," or "I asked her to my party, but when she gave one at the country club I didn't get asked." A vast body of information of that sort indicates just where the bonds of close social intimacy lie in a community.

You would be surprised—or at least I was (I was skeptical of all this stuff at first)—how much the problem does tend to pattern out.

There are of course some individual cases that you cannot, except purely arbitrarily, place; but I was so skeptical of this that I said to some of my students: "Well, this may work in the South and in some static Eastern communities, but take a frontier town like

[4] Op. cit.

VI. Student — Teacher

one I know very well, Gallup, in New Mexico, and don't tell me there are six social classes in Gallup."

So I started some of my students to work on this. We did not do a complete job, but we took the local papers and studied and tabulated and grouped who invited whom to parties and all that sort of thing. We did some interviewing—enough so that I saw that I was wrong; that, completely contrary to my preconceptions, even in Gallup, New Mexico, there was a pattern. In Gallup you can distinguish fairly consistently six different social classes. I had to be beaten by the facts to accept that point of view.

As to percentages, I will have to quote from memory, and they will be only roughly correct. They may not even be that, but they won't be too far off. I do not think anybody is in a position to give facts for the country as a whole, but in one community of about thirty thousand people Warner's figures [5] go something like this: upper-upper, 1.4 per cent; lower-upper, 1.6 per cent; upper-middle, 10 per cent; lower-middle, 28 per cent; upper-lower, about 25 per cent; lower-lower, 34 per cent.

[5] Ibid.

VII

FRIEND — FRIEND

by JOHN A. P. MILLET, M.D.[1]

FRIENDSHIP, the relation of friend to friend, might be looked upon as the basic example of human interrelationship. If we are not a good friend to our father, or to the postman, or to the neighbor across the street, or to the President or maybe the King of England, we are not extending the possibilities of friendship that we have, for we could be friends to any or all of them.

A definition of friendship has been attempted by philosophers, orators, poets, artists of all kinds. There is hardly a play of Shakespeare's in which there is not somebody called "friend to Hamlet," or "friend to—" somebody else, as you well remember, so that the stereotype of the friend is a favorite topic for writers of all kinds.

Poets and philosophers give us very often, through their intuitive insights, understanding about the relationships in life, about happenings on this good planet of ours. Since each person's individual experience must be very limited, we can get a good deal of insight from familiarity with the classics, with the poets and philosophers, the novelists, dramatists, and essayists. They can be considered as the challengers to better understanding, the expounders of problems, and the artists

[1] Harvard. Associate Attending Psychoanalyst, College of Physicians and Surgeons, Columbia University.

VII. Friend — Friend

of intuitive insight. They can increase our understanding of the interpersonal relationship of friendship. But perhaps, since this problem of how we can be better friends to more people is obviously right now one of the world's major problems, psychiatry has the responsibility and the ability to make its contribution toward understanding and building friendship.

Psychiatry makes its best contributions in the field of human relations when it works side by side with other social scientists—psychologists, clergymen, educators, anthropologists, and historians. This interdiscipline group draws upon the workers in the great human laboratories of the world. There may be hope that their discoveries will yield more to the development of a better integrated society than has come so far from the often repeated expositions, admonitions, and warnings of their more vocal brethren whose laboratory is the study and whose materials are ideas.

Goethe has a little something to say that applies to the contributions of both groups. He said: "In the arts and sciences, in addition to this close association among their votaries, a relation to the public is as favorable as it is necessary. Whatever of universal interest one thinks or accomplishes belongs to the world, and the world brings to maturity whatever it can utilize of the efforts of the individual."

For the moment I will swap places and ape the armchair philosophers (even though to my regret I can be neither orator nor poet) while giving my definition of friendship before speaking as a psychiatrist.

Our friend is one whose coming always brings pleasure, and whose going is always a source of regret. He is one whose welfare and happiness are matters of enduring concern. If they are threatened we feel anxiety, as though the danger were threatening ourselves, and our thoughts are bent chiefly on eliminating the threat or on bringing what help we can if the threat becomes a reality. If the frailties of human nature are on occasion exemplified in some measure in his person, our privilege is then to understand him even better than before. What our habitual judgment may consider to be a weakness or a failing does not need to be the reason for our valuing our friend less highly, or for considering that he has in some way betrayed us. On the contrary, it may make us wonder the more that this friend has attained such worth despite this apparent contradiction in his nature. It may make us more satisfied with his basic humanity, and more conscious of the fact that he is more like ourself and therefore more entitled to our sympathetic consideration. Through the greater freedom in communication which this insight makes possible we may expect to be of greater help in such a crisis.

Friendship is not soluble in the fluids of space and time: the measure of its constitution is not quantitative, but qualitative. It requires certain basic elements in its structure if it is to become really a firm cement that binds people more strongly with the years, rather than some kind of ersatz substance that permits weakening or collapse when unexpected stresses threaten the structure.

This structure of friendship is indeed no less than society itself, for society is founded on the more or less voluntary association of individual with individual and of group with group. Its supporting basement is that strange admixture of needs and resultant drives

VII. Friend — Friend

which compose the dynamics of the human organism. The ground floor is the family; the second floor, the school; the third, fourth, fifth, and sixth floors are the occupational setting, the community, the state, and the nation. The penthouse is the international community, whose architects cannot seem to agree on either the supports, the materials to be used, the height to which it must rise, or the builders who could be trusted to execute a perfect design.

Now if we turn to the consideration of friendships reared out of materials we can call ersatz, we must begin to speak somewhat in psychological terms, from the standpoint of the scientist.

First of these ersatz materials is what you might describe as over-flexible or over-labile tendencies to emotional attraction. The attraction comes easily; the attraction leaves easily. Some people are so constituted that they have a great sudden feeling of goodness toward some person they meet. We remember the song in *South Pacific*, "Some Enchanted Evening." That might be described as a bit of folk music bearing on this idea. But there are for some people many enchanted evenings. They pass from one enchanted evening to another. The result is that what seems to be a very promising beginning of friendship soon lapses into a mere incident of short duration and of little value—a good example of "easy come, easy go."

Scientifically we might label this, but I don't want to get into the libido theory. Let's call it, in simple terms, a tendency to easy attraction to other human objects, this ease of attraction being paralleled by the ease with which the attraction drops away.

The second of these ersatz materials is perhaps the

most important one of all: the expectation of gratifying unresolved, unsatisfied infantile needs that have survived though one has grown to be an adult. We all of us have some unsatisfied infantile needs. Those that we have are exactly the things in us which make us trying to the majority of our fellow human beings. A determined and continuing expectation of gratifying our surviving infantile needs is based on or leads to urges and drives that are no longer appropriate to the design the individual has for himself in life at the adult period. Furthermore, the conflict between such infantile drives—remaindermen, as we call them—and the more genuine rational needs of the organism is obviously such that the rational part of the human being cannot get on with the business of living, or get on toward the goals he is seeking.

Another type of ersatz material is the opportunistic attitude, the attitude that makes one look for friends who will push one along a peg higher, perhaps, and that leads to thinking of friends only in these self-interested terms. I am sure you have heard a great many people accused rather contemptuously of having such tendencies. It is highly probable that we all have that mechanism in us to some degree. A little boy who wants a bit of candy in the middle of the morning says to his mother: "Can't I have a bit of candy?" Being told: "No, you know perfectly well you can't have any candy until after lunch," he will run out and see an aunt on the lawn and say to his aunt: "Auntie, can't I go and get your scissors?" Auntie becomes a stepping-stone toward getting that candy in the middle of the morning.

That is not confined to children either; in general,

VII. Friend — Friend

the opportunistic attitude might be described as one of the important ersatz materials in the structure of friendship.

A somewhat related ersatz is that which causes people to seek the type of partnership in groups where the aim is self-aggrandizement and the development or maintenance of power and privilege. They will settle for the aggrandizement of the group as a kind of extension of their own personal needs which could not possibly be achieved without the support of and the identification with the group.

There are certainly other ersatz materials used in erecting the structure of friendship, but these are the principal ones that make for shaky structures. We might better turn our attention to the materials of personality that are best suited to the development of enduring friendship.

First of all, the soil of personality must have been fertilized by the experience of being loved sufficiently in childhood to make possible the wish to love others. That is to say, in general, to people who have had that fortunate experience, human beings appear benign rather than threatening. Their soil is fertilized for a good response when they meet another human being on the street.

Secondly, a sufficiently strong development of the ego. Here I have to digress for a minute to say that by ego I mean that part of the personality which has to mediate between one's emotional needs and the world of reality in which one lives. It is that part of the personality in which are lodged both our perceptions of the world in which we live and our recognition of pressures arising from inner needs, which express themselves as urges to action. The ego, furthermore, is the deliberative organ of our mental government. Like our own Congress, it is besieged by demands from a number of lobbies and is forced to make compromises that will not result in profligate action or spiritual bankruptcy. It has its own materials to work with, the stored impressions of past experience. Just as in a well-ordered department store the floor-walker will direct his customer to the proper department, so the ego refers each new situation to the appropriate section in its storehouse of experience to discover the goods that are needed to meet the demands of the situation. Thus it becomes the organ on which we must rely for the most reasonable reactions of which we are capable. Through its expanding controls it becomes our chief agent for meeting whatever challenge is offered by a constantly changing reality.

Everybody has a lot of opposites in him. We all have hate and love, aggressive tendencies and submissive tendencies, and social tendencies and antisocial tendencies, isolationist and group drives, and so forth and so on, all working from below on us to try to make us listen to what they are saying. The ego has to struggle with its resolution of these problems that beat upon it from below—that is, from the subconscious. If it does this with increasing success, it becomes better able to cope with all kinds of problems, both its own inner problems and problems that come at it from the outer world. A sufficiently strong ego development to resolve these basic conflicts as they come along, to handle the more aggressive and hostile tendencies, is able to clear the traffic lanes for the more positive, or what we speak of in psychological language as the

VII. Friend — Friend

erotic, drives. I am not using *erotic* to mean strongly sensual; *erotic* has a much broader meaning than that. It involves all the tendencies to feel toward and with other people, and is derived from the Greek word *Eros*, which is the name of a very pleasant god.

A third type of sound personality material is an insight into the infantile demands that we were talking about, sufficient to afford quick recognition of their appearance in the consciousness and to refuse them the right of way.

The fourth of these good materials that can make for sound friendships is respect for the self in its efforts to comprehend and accept the demands of reality and to make an appropriate adjustment to them. That comes largely from learning how to respect oneself. If we don't have respect for ourselves, how can we suppose the poor old self can go about making the adjustment of respecting other selves or expecting them to respect him? We need to have a good feeling toward ourself, in other words. It is a commonplace to say that you must love yourself before you can love anybody else, but within limits it is true. Of course, it can be carried too far. I know some people so concerned with loving themselves that they have nothing left for loving others.

Then out of this respect for oneself comes a corresponding respect for others, which ensures to them their right to have different feelings, different convictions, and different interests or aims from our own. A readiness to grant that one's opinions may be based on acquired prejudices and to listen with an open mind to another's viewpoint is a further requisite. We need, too, a growing ability to sift the wheat from the chaff in the value systems to which individuals adhere, and to stand by those values which have basic and predominant importance for oneself.

Another very important requisite in friendship is the ability to recognize the infantile demands not only in oneself but also in other people, and to face the impossibility of gratifying those demands unless one is willing to be chained somehow to a continuing process of having to gratify them.

This being impossible, it is not well for the ego to get involved, because the ego supposedly deals with reality and not with impossibility. The invasion of one's own province of interest and time by the infantile demands of others tends to breed resentment and to block free expression of good feelings in more appropriate directions.

On the other hand, it is equally necessary to recognize that one must accept the fact of interdependence with other people as a necessity for personal growth. We cannot grow up as human beings in a vacuum; we actually have to depend on others for the fulfillment of various needs that we have. The human being is a social animal. When he wants to get away and live by himself in isolation, it is because he is sick; it is not because he wants to add one more brick to the House of Wisdom. This implies a responsibility for defining to oneself the purpose of every interpersonal relationship and the extent to which one is willing and able to cultivate it.

What basic dynamics go into the development of the human being so that he can use these materials that we have been talking about for the building of this structure of friendship?

VII. *Friend — Friend*

First of all, the human being starts as a totally inexperienced creature. His first experience is purely sensory, mostly uncomfortable. He gets some relief when he gets a good meal, but for a long time he isn't able to differentiate himself from the world of objects and people around him.

That is the great time of life for each of us. Then we are the complete imperialist; all we have to do is squeal, and somebody rushes and does something or undoes something, and we relax again. We don't have to work again until the next time we experience discomfort.

Following this early-infancy state of imperialism comes the gradual differentiation of the self from the world around, the "I" and the "Not I," and eventually, of course, the gradual realization of the importance and size of other people—how powerful they are, how they can do anything they want: pick you up, throw you down, put you in water, take you out of the water, feed you or not feed you. It is quite obvious very early that we are bound to be affected by a sense of difference in respect to other people.

First of all we think we are the whole world, if you like. Then gradually we find that there are other cheeses around us, and those cheeses get bigger and bigger for a while. This is perhaps basically the origin of that sense of difference which leads to the danger of hostility reactions between human beings, and difficulties in the creating of friendships.

But in view of this great problem of the power and sometimes the arrogance of adults around the child, he has to begin to make some compromises, and he finds that he cannot get things unless he gives something to these people—unless he smiles when they come into the room, or coos, or conforms when he is having his toilet training, or whatever it may be. He has to make some kind of gift in order to retain the goodwill of the powerful adult. *Quid pro quo* comes in.

Here is the beginning of friendship, the surrender of some part of that complete love of self to another person who meets his needs. If the child has a good enough experience through those years to discover that these mighty powers are, on the whole, benign powers, and he goes out into the company of mates of his own age armed, so to speak, with a certain assurance, a certain basic unconscious optimism about life, then he will at once begin to seek out relationships with his fellow children and to rattle down gradually to some place where he finds acceptance. Through seeking association with those he finds to be like himself he has a phantasy of doubling or trebling the strength of his ego.

He next gets interested in team play. He subordinates his egoistic demands on the team to the work of the team as a whole. Just because he happens to run faster and play right end, he doesn't have to be given the ball every single play. And he learns that sometimes it is better perhaps that the half-back carry the ball through left tackle.

If this subordination is successfully accomplished, he discovers the joy of sharing experience with others, the actual feeling of being a part of a team rather than an individual struggling for recognition all by himself. So he repeats this satisfaction by becoming part of other groups.

VII. Friend — Friend

Then comes the emergence of some kind of feeling of social role. He feels he has some kind of position in the world, that his role in society might be this or might be that. He begins to get a sense of real identity; and his discovery of satisfactions, the emergence of his own identity, and his feeling of confidence in his personal relationships develop a really new ability to crystallize aims, purposes, plans, and to proceed toward goals in a fairly reasonable manner.

Among those goals, of course, is the creating and making of new relationships, the making of new friends.

It is rather fun to imagine to oneself how the original primitive friendship might have started. I think it is probable that two boys came out of two caves and saw the same lion, and that they had a race to see who would get there first. The first fellow stuck his spear in, and just as he did so, the second fellow came along and was just about to stick his spear in the first fellow when the lion turned around and clawed him, whereupon he got angry with the lion and stuck the spear in the lion. Well, they both got some kind of surprised reaction. The first boy was already angry at the lion, the second got angry at the lion, so they both went after the lion until the lion got killed. Then they started to go after each other, and each suddenly realized that the same thing he was planning to do to the other one might happen to him, and so they somehow decided they would split up the lion or drag it off and eat it together.

Some such occasional experience as that was probably what gave man the idea of dividing his loyalties between himself and somebody else—in other words, of the need of mutual support or sharing. In union there is strength. From that, man's social relationships have progressed from family to tribe to nation.

If we review some of the definitions of friendship given by the philosophers, we find they illustrate aptly a few of these points.

Emerson, for instance, defines the essence of friendship as "entireness, a total magnanimity and trust. . . . It treats its object as a god, that it may deify both."

An Australian soldier, a more modern and homespun philosopher, was greeted in a bar by one of my friends during the war. After having a few glasses of beer, they got into a philosophic discussion. The Australian soldier talked about what good friends the Australians were with the Americans, and said: "We're very much like you, you know. We are friends."

And my friend asked: "Well, what is a friend? What do you mean by a friend?"

"Well, a friend is sometimes above you and he is sometimes below you, but he's always beside you."

Going much farther back, to Cicero and his essay *De amicitia—On Friendship*—we find some of the best discussion of the origins of friendship. At one point in that three-way dialogue Cicero has Fannius saying: "I gather that friendship springs from a natural impulse rather than a wish for help; from an inclination of the heart combined with a certain instinctive feeling of love rather than from a deliberate calculation of the material advantage it was likely to confer."

What is ego identification? Recognizing somebody with whom you can identify yourself, somebody not exactly the same as you but having certain sympathetic

VII. Friend — Friend

qualities that you would like to have and perhaps do have in some measure but sense in greater amount in the other fellow. We call that ego identification. Emerson recognizes its importance in friendship when he says: "I must feel pride in my friend's accomplishments as if they were mine."

All of us have ideals, we all have consciences with greater or less influences on our life, and many of us feel that we can never attain or live up to what our consciences demand of us. We have an ideal for ourselves, an ego ideal, but it is a hard job keeping pace with it. So a friend has this peculiar value to a man: that the man can project this conscience of his, this ideal fellow, onto his friend and let him carry the ball. Then he can admiringly say to himself: "That is a wonderful fellow," thinking about all the other fellow's virtues, forgetting all about his own problem with his own ego ideal.

On this Emerson says: "We over-estimate the conscience of our friend. His goodness seems better than our goodness, his nature finer, his temptation less."

It is very probable that he feels the same about us, you see, and that is why it is possible for two people to be friends. The stature of the ego, of the self, is enormously enhanced through the relations of friendship. Very often, in talking with somebody you like very much, you suddenly find yourself becoming so much better, so much more cheerful than you realized you were before. Emerson spotted that and said: "We are made brighter, more free in expression, in the presence of a friend."

Bacon is the most delightful writer on the subject. If you are really interested in learning something about the relation of friend to friend, I advise you to get out Bacon's essay "Of Friendship."

Again, on the great need for preserving the independence of the self within a friendship, which I indicated was among the basic materials for a sound structure of friendship, Emerson has some very pertinent things to say. He writes:

"The only joy I have in his being mine is that the 'not mine' is 'mine.' . . . There must be very two before there can be very one. . . . We must be our own before we can be another's. . . .

"Leave it to girls and boys to regard a friend as property, and to such a short and all confounding pleasure, instead of the pure nectar of God. . . .

"You shall not come nearer to a man by coming into his house."

That is not merely a physical statement—going in the front door of a friend's house. It means trying to get into his innermost thoughts and feelings and not leaving any little tiny corner to himself. It suggests the idea of trying to possess a person's whole mind, so that there is not a single corner of it with which you are not familiar. This approach, of course, makes a complete prisoner of the other person and in no way promotes your own development, because it is not your mind then you are trying to capture but the other person's. "Friendship requires that rare mean betwixt likeness and unlikeness that piques each with the presence of power and of consent in the other party."

The new idiom for friendship today that we can derive from some of these considerations is not easy to define. What I have tried to indicate here is that as the philosophers have *described* friendship, so science

VII. Friend — Friend

has investigated its structure in terms of the psychological relation of the child to the adult, of the child to the child, and of the adult to the adult, and of the individual to the group.

There are some very important measurements of group relations going on at the University of Michigan at the present time. They have been given great importance in the industrial field—by management and also by students. We are going to learn a lot more in a scientific way about individual and group relations as a result of such studies, and I hope we shall put what we learn to work.

Since the primary identification with others is what draws people together, the task of parents, educators, and social scientists is to find new techniques for breaking down barriers of isolationism founded on the fear of being different. Difference is an essential of human nature, whether in individuals or in groups. The hope of the future is that scientific knowledge, the dynamics of individual development and of various cultures, may lead to the better patterning of family and group relations.

The human race has come a long way, but it is unquestionably at the crossroads. The need for recognizing friendship as the symbol of a new way was never greater. A new generation trained and educated under the banner of modern psychology, whose aim is to eliminate the brakes that are put on the fullest expression of those drives which bring men together, and to find improved methods for the mastery of destructive tendencies, would of necessity demand an extension of the fronts of communication without which no increase in the front of friendship is possible.

This is today's challenge. How can we learn to make more friends within our own borders? How can we learn to communicate with one another right here? How can we learn, in our Congress or in the United Nations, to communicate with one another? We have to learn to make better friends with our own groups in our own bailiwick first of all or we can't be friends on a national or international level.

The limits to friendship are set by anxiety, whether between individuals or groups. The reality of interdependence, while intellectually acknowledged, is emotionally resisted. The strength of this resistance is roughly proportional to the size and power of the social unit. One man can get over a bad or a difficult feeling in relation to one person more easily than can fifteen people get over a bad feeling about another fifteen people. The problem becomes bigger and bigger as the size of the group increases.

The science of psychodynamics came into being when the techniques of scientific inquiry and careful documentation were applied to the investigation of the mental field of individual human beings. Its more recent extension to the study of individuals in their group settings has already added much to the sum total of our understanding of human society. As the science of motivation, it has fertilized new fields of research in the allied sciences of anthropology and sociology. These sciences in their turn have enriched the science of psychodynamics by presenting unsolved problems in the field of group interactions and mass psychology. Thus an alliance between dynamic psychology and the social sciences offers a new and fruitful approach to the solution of all problems in the field

VII. Friend — Friend

of group relations, from those familiar in the family to those less familiar and more perplexing in the field of international relations. The time has come when a more friendly ear might well be lent by those entrusted with the making of national and international policy to such insights into their problems as might be provided by this already effective alliance.

I met a very distinguished national figure from another country not so very long ago who had been in the political arena for some twenty-five or thirty years. He said that he wanted to devote the remainder of his life to introducing the known facts of psychological and social science into the political structure of society. He is the top man of one of the delegations to the United Nations, and this is his credo today. So I think that these statements have fairly good support in other areas than the psychiatric field. But we need more and more men each in his own sphere making these same applications of the principles of sound friendship if we are ever to build the penthouse of human relations.

1. Will you please comment on this quotation I recently heard made by a famous novelist: "Psychiatry cannot make a warm heart if it just isn't there."

Certainly one cannot create something out of nothing; but what often passes for the absence of a warm heart is a terror of expressing warm feelings that has been so inculcated in an individual from childhood on, because of rebuffs and rejections, that even the individual himself does not know that he has any warm feelings.

In situations like that, provided the individual is not a very sick person, it is often possible to bring out those feelings from underneath. Naturally, there are some people who have been so injured, so traumatized by life, that scars are left; but that is frequently a reversible condition, if I may put it that way. The warm heart is there if you have the skill to peel off the layers of protective coating.

2. Isn't the best friend a person who knows how to listen when a friend has problems, rather than try to give advice, only to say too much or too little and be thoroughly disliked in the end?

I should say the latter part of that question was a good statement of what a friend is not. This would be like going to your headmaster and being told where to get off. This is not ordinarily a situation in which a friend likes to find himself.

Certainly the art of listening to somebody else is an essential part of the relationship. If *you* talked all the time, there wouldn't be much relationship. On the other hand, if you never answered, that wouldn't be much of a relationship either. There should be an exchange of comment at least. A friend is more than just a good listener.

VII. *Friend — Friend* [201

3. **Please elucidate what constitutes infantile needs to be recognized as unworthy elements in the structure of friendship.**

These infantile needs are frequently shown in outbursts of anger over trifling frustrations, tantrums that in early childhood may have been found to be an effective technique for either getting attention or getting one's own way. Overdependence on others for advice and comfort when facing a perplexing situation, and possessive jealousy of other people's attention and affection might be cited as other examples. Excessive absorption with reports on the sports pages, college football as another device for avoiding adult realities, and the habit of making the unexpected appearance of an old friend the occasion for going on a bender—these are all types of infantile hangovers.

4. **Is it possible to revive a lost friendship if you consider it worthy? How?**

My answer to that is: if you have a friendship, you never really lose it. You may think or believe you have a friendship, and it may depart from you; but there was something that was ersatz in that friendship if that happens.

If you think there has been a misunderstanding and you have met some unexpected kind of response you don't understand, in what is and always has been a good friendship, it is your responsibility toward that friend to go and say: "Hey! What's the matter with you? What did you say that for?" or "What do you think of me?" or something that can start to clear up the difficulty and restore proper values in the relationship.

In other words, you have to show some ingenuity at times in keeping a friendship going, just as when you light a fire and the wood is damp, you have to use some ingenuity in keeping the blaze going.

5. Why is it possible to get along for years with tradespeople, servants at home, yet be unsuccessful in relationships with friends and relatives?

That is indeed a very common, a much too common problem. The main fundamental reason is that the early relationships were never on a sound footing, or else for some reason your particular relatives were particularly disagreeable and hostile people. Which is also a possibility.

But it more usually goes back to the relationship developed in childhood between the child and the parents, and then not being helped over the bump of making adjustments in school, and getting into the pattern of good close relationships.

After all, it is to some extent a one-way relationship with tradespeople and with people who help in your work at home. They are more dependent on you in certain ways than you are on them. On the other hand, in other ways you are more dependent on them than they are on you. You couldn't get along without groceries, though you could get the same groceries at some other place. More likely, if you lose a cleaning woman who has become a successful addition to your

VII. *Friend — Friend*

household, you perhaps are rather more dependent on her than she is on you. It turns the tables a bit. But in neither of these situations is there the more complex interpersonal relationship that is involved in day-by-day living with friends and relatives.

6. What does psychiatry tell us about how individuals choose their friends?

Friends usually begin by happenstance. You don't say: "Today I'm going out to choose a friend." It results from a series of very complicated operations in our central nervous system. Perhaps we smell the person's perfume, we'll say, or see a pretty face or a kind smile, or we hear a pleasant voice. We feel an attraction toward that person. We want to talk to him. Then communication begins, and maybe he starts talking about ideas that sound extraordinarily like our ideas. That is wonderful! And we want to hear much more about them. We make a date for dinner the next day, and so on.

In other words, it goes first from the sense organs to the feelings, then finally up into the cortex, where there is association of ideas and thought, and eventually may go up into the more ethereal layers of the cortex where ideals are lodged, the higher elements of personality, where the purpose of friendship is clearly perceived and where thoughtful attention is given to it.

7. Should parents influence children in the choice of friends?

That is a little like asking whether an apple should fall off the tree. They can't help influencing their children in the choice of friends. The children smell their parents' approval or disapproval if not a word is spoken, and if not a word is spoken they usually know just so much more than if much is said.

So in general I think the rational answer to a question like that is that children should be encouraged in every possible way to discover ways of making friends on their own, and that parents should interfere with a continuation of a friendship only if it seems to develop in ways not altogether desirable.

8. The ability to experience friendship is limited by anxiety. Will you please explain?

If you had no fear of what might happen to you if you made a continuing and close contact with another human being, you would have no difficulty in making a relationship with that person. There might be all kinds of reasons why you fear continuing relations with that person. I don't need to challenge your imaginations on that.

What I meant by saying that friendship is limited by anxiety is that anxiety leads to a person holding himself from contact with other people, usually because he has had some bad experiences at some time during his development, and he loses his freedom of intercourse with other people.

It does not mean that you should be completely

VII. *Friend — Friend*

anxiety-free in relation to contacts with other human beings, of course. If you saw a fellow walking around a dark alley with his hand in his pocket, you might anticipate that there was to be some shooting very shortly. The anticipation might not be directed toward you, but you would have some anxiety. You wouldn't pat him on the back and say: "Old chap, don't you think you'd better give me that gun?"

There are certain types of anxiety in relation to contacts with other human beings which have at least a possibility of rational confirmation. But what anxiety does is to limit the freedom of personal intercourse and to limit the possibility of understanding between people.

9. What do you think of the theory that if you have one true friend in your lifetime, you are indeed fortunate?

I think that "one true friend" is a little pessimistic. I think one might hope with reasonably decent behavior and a good friendly outlook toward humanity to collect, say, half a dozen. Be on the optimistic side.

10. From definite trends in friends which we observe in our adolescent children, can we sometimes find signs of emotional instability that should be understood and then aided?

"From definite trends in friends which we observe in our adolescent children"—in other words,

I think it means this: we notice that our children turn toward certain kinds of friends. Can we sometimes find signs of emotional instability? Yes, that certainly is true. If there is a general tendency to make friends of only one sort, and particularly when that one sort is exaggerated in its attitude in any particular direction (such as taking on some pattern of political thinking, or very prejudicial attitudes, or running after big names, autograph-hunting in an adult form), that is likely to be a signal of some kind of trouble, not necessarily serious, but calling for a little professional advice.

11. What about platonic friendship between the sexes? Does it really exist?

Why of course it really exists! The relation of a friendship between two people of the same sex may be just exactly as important as a friendship between two people of opposite sexes. There may be, both between people of opposite sexes and between people of the same sex, a wish to get out of a friendship certain things they are no longer entitled to because these things are infantile hangovers. But there are such things as adult males and adult females, and between an adult man and an adult woman there can be friendship that is platonic, with no dark and hidden and bad designs of some character, presumably sexual.

VII. Friend — Friend

12. Does the intellect play a major, a minor, or a negligible role in friendship?

Certainly the intellect is not negligible. It sometimes plays a major role and sometimes a minor one. If some of the materials of friendship between people are those of intellectual exchange—take for instance two professors at a university, if you like, or a man and a wife both of whom are artists or poets, or two friends both of whom are engrossed in the study of atomic fission and who live together while working in the same laboratory—the intellect may play a very important part in such a relationship, because it enriches the ready medium of exchange.

The intelligence—as opposed to intellect—plays a very important part, because the intelligence, which is what we might call our steering wheel, helps us to understand what is going on and to take steps to be on guard.

13. What is the role of homosexuality in the relationship between friend and friend?

If you call an affectionate feeling toward somebody of your own sex a sexual feeling, then you can say there is homosexuality implied in that relation. Indulging in certain physical acts that are ordinarily part of the sexual relation goes beyond affectionate feelings and their exchange.

It all depends, really, on the definition of the word *sexual*. You see, we often confuse *sexual* with *genital* in our language. It is one of these semantic problems. The sexual instinct involves a whole lot of other organs than the genital organs. The eye is a sexual organ —the nose, the mouth, the skin, and so on. There isn't a single sense that is not involved in the total picture of the sexual instinct. So that if you think of sexuality as including every sensory reaction that is pleasurable, it could be said that in many relationships between people of the same sex where there is no physical contact of the genital type, or anything that approaches it, there is some homosexuality.

You may like your friend's voice; you may like to look at the clothes he wears, and so on. It is dangerous to let yourself think in such terms, because you are starting out with a stereotyped notion of what homosexuality is.

It would be better if we had such a word in common use perhaps as *homofilial* instead of *homosexual*.

VIII

EMPLOYER — EMPLOYEE

by LEO H. BARTEMEIER, M.D.[1]

It is my intention to discuss the relationship of the employer and the employee in the light of my professional training and my clinical experience. I can serve no useful purpose by speculating and theorizing about the larger industrial problems that threaten our national security because these problems are beyond my personal competence. I will limit my remarks, therefore, to the knowledge psychiatry has contributed to this important question of the employer and the employee. I shall use the term *employer* to include all persons who stand in authority over the worker and who may be actual employers or representatives of the ultimate employer. These persons include foremen, department heads, managers, superintendents, supervisors, and so on.

The problems connected with the employer-employee relationship are numerous, complex, and important for a variety of reasons. They are important because of the very large number of persons who are involved. Over sixty million of our people are employed, and one or two members of each family are working at jobs. Moreover, eight and one-fourth mil-

---

[1] Georgetown. Associate Professor of Psychiatry, College of Medicine, Wayne University; president, International Psychoanalytic Association.

lion women were employed in 1948 in contrast with two million in 1940. The relationship between employers and employees is important also because it is a health problem of considerable magnitude that affects a much larger number of persons than those who are actually employed. A father who is chronically discontented with his job creates an emotionally unhealthy climate in his family. This may be reflected in his child's poor report card or in some of the distress for which his wife consults the family physician. The satisfaction and sense of well-being which the head of a family derives from his work has a healthy and wholesome effect on the lives of his wife and his children because the morale of the family hinges so sensitively on the spirit of its leader.

It is now generally recognized that causes of disease are not to be found simply in physical and biological factors. Economic and social conditions increasingly are seen to play an important part in health problems. When the sixty-four countries signed the constitution of the World Health Organization in New York three years ago, they promulgated the principle that "Health is a state of complete physical, mental, and social well-being, and not merely the absence of disease or infirmity." An employee may be physically robust and muscularly strong enough to do twice the amount of work his job requires, but if he cannot get along with his foreman the tension that he repeatedly experiences during his working day not only interferes with his efficiency but may be the cause of his insomnia, his lowered resistance to infection, and his irritability with his wife and his children. His work performance may be satisfactory so far as his foreman

VIII. *Employer — Employee*

is concerned, but an unsatisfactory employer-employee relationship activates something that is unhealthy within him, and we would be correct in saying that he is not in good health.

A worker who expresses dissatisfaction with his job may be unsuited for the specific kind of work in which he is engaged, but his work includes not only the job itself but also the persons *with* whom he works and the person or firm *for* whom he works. Most jobs necessarily involve a foreman, a department head, a supervisor, or some other figure of authority to whom the worker is responsible, to whom he must account for what he is doing, and with whom he has a continuing relationship. My clinical observations repeatedly demonstrate that the relationship of the employee to his employer is at least as important as the actual work he performs and that the two cannot be regarded separately. They are the two aspects of a total situation. In most instances it turns out that how well or how poorly the employee and his employer get along with each other is of greater importance to the employee than the job itself. What his boss thinks of him, how he feels about him, how he behaves toward him, provide incentives for a great many employees to work happily and efficiently at jobs for which they would have no incentives were the emotional satisfactions of these relationships withdrawn. I have often heard a man say: "I used to love my job; it was interesting and I seldom missed a day at my bench. But it's different now; I've become bored with it—it's just something I *have* to do." In many of these instances it was plain to see that changes had occurred in the employees' relations with their supervisors and that these changes were responsible for their loss of interest in their work. In some instances these men had lost their supervisors, in others the quality of their relationships with them had changed. With all of them their attitude toward themselves and toward their jobs had undergone unfavorable consequences which resulted in a poorer work performance and therefore an economic loss to the industries that employed them.

The morale of a group of workers also is important for the satisfactions that workers derive from their jobs. Good group morale provides them with sustained incentives for their productivity. When the group morale is high we invariably find that the quality of leadership by the foreman of the department is good and that the emotional bonds with his men are consistently strong. This is the team spirit that accounts for a high rate of efficiency and productivity of workers. In his book *Psychiatry in a Troubled World*, Dr. William C. Menninger states that "Morale most often becomes a matter of concern in wartime, but it is equally important to the attitudes and feelings of any group of workers in an industrial or business organization. The Army psychiatrist became acutely sensitive to the factors that influenced it. The incidence of mental ill health made him aware of the inadequacy of leadership. He saw the effect on morale of leadership which had an appreciation of the personal factors that make life rich or lean. Failure of leadership was related most often to this lack of recognition of and concern about the individual." [2]

The quality of the relationship between the em-

[2] William C. Menninger: *Psychiatry in a Troubled World* (New York: Macmillan Co.; 1948), p. 498.

VIII. *Employer — Employee*

ployee and his employer which so strongly influences a man's attitude and his feelings about his job may be compared to the first work every human being performs during the period of infancy. Eating constitutes the first expenditure of muscular energy that results in fatigue, and anyone observing a nursing infant cannot fail to be impressed by the work that taking food involves. We know that how easily the infant takes his food and how well he digests it are precisely determined by the quality of his relationship with his mother. If the relationship is one in which he feels secure and protected and loved, he likes his food, takes it readily, and digests it well. It is now well established that his health is largely connected with what he feels and the way he feels about his mother. If he feels rejected and insecure, he loses his interest in his food and either does not take it well or vomits it, or develops colic or other digestive disturbances. These facts are well understood by pediatricians who recognize the importance of the mother's understanding of her baby's needs and the satisfactions he requires for optimum growth and development. Work and the boss are associated in adult life as intimately as are food and the mother in the infantile period.

Those who are employed need something more than jobs to perform and pay checks for doing them. A "strictly businesslike" attitude on the part of the employer toward the employee, which means a rather impersonal attitude and one that is quite devoid of feeling, can never result in a good performance by the worker. If it is true that man does not live by bread alone, and I think that each of you will agree with me that this *is* true, then by the same token no employee can consistently do his job well without those emotional satisfactions he gets from his boss or from belonging to the group of fellow workers with whom he identifies himself. It is one thing for a foreman to reprimand a worker or threaten him because he is not doing enough work or he is doing it improperly, and another thing for him to inquire of the worker if he is not feeling well or if he is worried about something. It often happens that temporary inefficiency on the job is the external manifestation of anxiety or of being sick in some other way.

I recall a worker who was preoccupied with acute concern over the sudden illness of his wife and the necessity of finding someone to look after his children. This so interfered with his work that his foreman gave him a sharp warning about losing his job. What he needed instead was immediate help with what was concerning him so deeply that it interfered with his work. Had he been sent to an emotional first-aid station where a professionally trained person could have advised him, his anxiety would have been lessened and his work efficiency would have improved at once.

In contrast with this incident, I well remember a worker in a furniture factory who had injured his hand and been treated by the doctor in the first-aid station. The physical injury was only slight, but the doctor was quick to see that the worker was excessively worried about his hand. Although he knew it was unnecessary, he suggested that the hand be X-rayed. Forthwith the employee was taken to a local physician in a cab and the picture was made. He was also told to take the rest of the day off with pay. The incident was typical of the attitude toward the workers in this

VIII. *Employer — Employee* [215

factory. It was a healthy organization with excellent morale and never had serious labor difficulties.

When we were children we did various kinds of work for our mothers and our fathers. We did those little jobs because we loved the pat on the back or the kiss on the cheek we received for doing them. We did them, too, sometimes because we were afraid to disobey and we wanted above all to avoid parental criticism and punishment. But more often we did our childish work in order to receive extra supplements of love and affection and approval of ourselves for having done them. In those days we did not work because we liked to or because we found satisfaction in work for its own sake. We worked to please our parents. We worked in order to get more love. It has been said that one of the differences between the child and the adult is that for the adult, work should be an end in itself; that work should provide a feeling of satisfaction through achievement in addition to the pay one receives for doing it. We know this is not always true. Much work is monotonous, repetitious, and boring. This is true even for the artist, the inventor, and many other creative workers. But it is also true that no one ever matures completely and that even the artist, the inventor, the designer, and the composer who have no employers and who work independently seem to need some praise, some recognition, some commendation for their achievements.

In an emotional sense, none of us ever *really* leave our fathers and mothers, no matter how wise we become or how maturely our personalities develop, or how much we achieve by way of leadership, responsibility, or life experience itself. We receive our education, we get married, we establish our own homes and become parents ourselves. We try to assume our responsibilities and develop a certain degree of independence. We participate in the affairs of our communities and do what we can toward contributing to the common good. And yet we never completely part with those feelings we experienced in connection with our parents when we were little children. They have disappeared from our awareness and have been buried in the deeper layers of our personalities.

These attitudes and feelings often reappear in some of our adult relationships. The situations especially likely to revive feelings formerly experienced toward our parents are those in which we become dependent upon someone else in a way that is important to us. The employment situation is one of these. In every employee's relationship to his employer there are varying quantities of emotion that belong to the original child-parent relationship. These emotions comprise both tender and hostile feelings that a worker formerly had toward his father. How intensely or how mildly these feelings exist depends on the extent to which they have been worked out during childhood. Many workers who as children were never permitted by their fathers to express any of the resentment they felt toward them are likely to experience a reactivation of these resentments toward their employers. This is especially probable if they come to feel that they are merely cogs in a machine and that what they are doing is not appreciated. These resurgences of unresolved conflicts from childhood which give rise to so many disturbed relationships between employees and their employers are usually not recognized for what

VIII. *Employer — Employee* [217

they are by the workers themselves. They may only be aware of feeling tense or uncomfortable and uneasy in the presence of their supervisors. These unrecognized feelings are the causative factors of some industrial accidents and errors, inefficiency on the job, violation of factory rules, absenteeism, and inability to hold positions. A man whose hatred of his father is unwittingly transferred to his employer repeatedly provokes him quite unintentionally. He goes from one job to another and is unable to remain continuously employed. Too often he is merely labeled a troublemaker and is discharged instead of being given the professional assistance he needs. In one study [3] of over 4,000 industrial cases, 62 per cent of discharges were because of social incompetence rather than technical incompetence. In the experience of Dr. V. V. Anderson,[4] 20 per cent of all employees were problem workers. They were referred for varied reasons: bad attitudes, upsetting the morale of a department, poor production, nervousness, chronic-illness complex, poor attendance record, being a constant disciplinary problem, resenting authority, wasting time, damaging goods. Dr. William C. Menninger [5] stated that these were essentially the same problems met with in the Army.

The reactivation of unfinished problems of childhood in the attitudes of employees toward their em-

[3] John M. Breiner: "Causes for Discharge," *Personnel Journal*, Vol. VI, pp. 171–2 (October 1, 1927).

[4] V. V. Anderson: "The Contribution of Mental Hygiene to Industry," *Readings in Mental Hygiene*, ed. by E. R. Groves and P. Blanchard (New York: Henry Holt & Co.; 1936), pp. 357–66.

[5] William C. Menninger, op. cit., p. 497.

ployers is a problem of vast importance in all business and industrial organizations. It is a problem that has been aggravated and intensified by technological progress and mass production with the consequent neglect of human needs and the ignoring of the necessity for human satisfactions in the employment situation. Dr. Karl A. Menninger [6] has pointed out that personal psychology has been so discredited in the entire set-up of industry, and the profit motive has been assumed to be so powerful and all-controlling, that satisfaction in work has come to be assessed entirely in terms of wages and hours, not only by employers but by employees themselves. Yet from the standpoint of psychology the recurring industrial and economic depressions might seem, in some degree, the result of profound dissatisfactions and disappointments in work, on the part of both employers and employees.

An extraordinarily important study of a small group of workers in the Western Electric Company was made by some psychologists.[7] For five years daily productivity was checked and compared with all sorts of conditions affecting the employees—their health, their working conditions, their home conditions, their attitudes, and their general morale. Of the many conclusions, the most pertinent is the fact that no matter what changes were made in the working conditions, in management techniques, in hours of labor, if the change was made with the manifest purpose of benefit-

[6] Karl A. Menninger: *Love against Hate* (New York: Harcourt, Brace & Co.; 1942), p. 140.

[7] J. F. Roethlisberger and William J. Dickson: *Management and the Worker* (Cambridge, Mass.: Harvard University Press; 1939).

VIII. *Employer — Employee* [219

ing the workers, efficiency and production were immediately and markedly stimulated. This demonstrates that fostering the affection of workers for an employer is more important than any specific concession or regulation because it permits more complete sublimation of the aggressive impulses that otherwise leak out in the form of resentment against the employer.

Men who are suffering from emotional disorders often tell us: "My father didn't understand me," "He didn't seem to care," "He was too busy," "He would punish me without trying to find out why I had done something." Everyone needs to feel that he counts; that what he does is appreciated or that it helps or is worth while, and that when he gives his best in his work, someone cares. Every employee needs to feel hopeful about his work and the possibility of advancing.

Doctors Thomas A. C. Rennie and Luther E. Woodward tell us that "Many leaders whose educational background and administrative experience have stressed technology and economics have found it hard to accept the provision of worker satisfactions as a legitimate and necessary function of industry but the number of voices demanding it is increasing at a more rapid rate than ever before. Leaders who are concerned with research into management and labor relations are stressing the importance of a practical knowledge of the social structure and of the psychological needs of workers, individually and in groups, as essential for sound management." [8] They point out that an indus-

[8] Thomas A. C. Rennie, M.D. and Luther E. Woodward, Ph.D.: *Mental Health in Modern Society* (New York: Commonwealth Fund; 1948), p. 275.

trial philosophy that regards technology and finance more real than human factors is a "truncated realism." "The administrator today requires, perhaps above all else, insight into the dynamics of human behavior, insight into the forces that make both for conflict and cooperation." It is necessary "to provide employees a socially significant way of life and maintain a condition of balance within the internal organization such that employees, by contributing their services, are able to justify their desires and hence are willing to cooperate.

"The concept that each man's potential in production is much higher than has generally been realized and that men are capable of great accomplishment and discipline when they share closely in a common enterprise under leaders whom they trust and admire proved its practical truth during the war. The time is ripe for its application to industry. Advocates of such a concept are not only psychologists, psychiatrists and social workers who were largely responsible for making it effective in military life, but also the businessmen and their advisors in the armed forces who saw it work and helped to make it work. The skilled personnel required to build up this esprit de corps in industry is to be found in substantial numbers among the veterans themselves, many of whom left the ranks of industry to join the army and have now returned to the same level of employment with an equipment for leadership which can be put to use. Their training and experience in understanding and managing people can readily be transferred to the industrial setting. Literature issued by industry to its management stresses the fact that veterans must be

VIII. *Employer — Employee* [221

assured in a practical way that industry is concerned with their personal welfare and happiness. At least one leaf has been taken from the book of the military psychiatrist and the morale services officer."

The British were so impressed with the improvement of their soldiers when consistent attention was given to building morale that at the end of the war they took most of the officers and enlisted men who had served in education and personnel work in the Army and set them to work in industrial plants. These veterans now train foremen to conduct group discussion, and, with the full knowledge and approval of top management, a certain amount of time each week is devoted to free discussion by the workers under the foreman's leadership. No subject is taboo and full and free expression is encouraged. Observers have reported an amazing degree of improvement in the workers' sense of participation and in the morale of entire plants. Similar work is going on in a few large corporations in this country. The human element in industry has been the concern of psychiatrists since 1919.

In a carefully conducted research by Dr. Russell Fraser [9] and his associates in England into the incidence of neurosis among factory workers, it was learned that as a cause of absence from work the incidence of neurotic illness was greater than that of the common cold. This research, which is one of the best of its kind to date, was sponsored by the Medical Research Council of Great Britain and involved the medical and psychological examination of over three

[9] Russell Fraser: *The Incidence of Neurosis among Factory Workers* (London: His Majesty's Stationery Office; 1947).

thousand workers in thirteen light and medium engineering factories. Both men and women workers were studied, and it was found over a period of two years that ten per cent of the workers suffered from a definite or disabling neurotic illness and that neurosis caused between a quarter and a third of the absences from work due to illness. Dr. Fraser concluded that "The effects of neurotic disability might be less than its overall incidence suggests, if it occurred mainly among the less productive and useful workers. In the factories studied, neurosis was as frequent among those on the more skilled as those on the less skilled jobs; and as frequent among those usually receiving the highest range of earnings as among those usually earning less. Therefore, failure to employ workers who suffer from neurotic illness, a practice that has been advocated in some quarters, would lead to wastage of the country's reservoir of skilled labor, and consequently of productive capacity."

Employees are employers' most valuable assets. When management consistently appreciates this fact and regards the workers as more important than the products of industry, the employer-employee relationship is healthy and the efficiency of workers is high. This has been demonstrated so often in the past that it constitutes the best guide for the future. Love is always more important to human beings than any wages they may earn.

VIII. *Employer — Employee*

1. Do you think it would be possible to have a mental first-aid station in every organization large enough to have a good medical program for its employees?

It will be possible as soon as industrial medical organizations develop the conviction that comprehensive medical care has become essential for protecting the health of employees and their families. Comprehensive medical care is that form of medical care which comprehends the patient as a person whose health is determined as much by his relations with his fellow workers, his foreman, his wife, and his children as by the infections or injuries he may experience. Mental health stations as facets of industrial medical organizations can alleviate the transitory emotional disturbances of many workers, can serve to maintain and promote the good health of workers and their families, and can spare much of the time of other members of the industrial medical staff, which is sorely needed for specific kinds of medical care they have been specially trained to administer. Mental first-aid stations should be under the direction of a psychiatrist, a clinical psychologist, and a psychiatric social worker. This professional team, functioning as part of the medical department in a large factory, provides the opportunity for rendering adequate medical care. In small factories a carefully selected social worker and a nurse can provide for the mental health needs of many workers seeking assistance.

**2. What can be done if your relationship with a supervisor is fine but your fellow workers are younger, immature, insolent to you, and put on a sweet front to the same supervisor?

The first thing to do is to recognize that the younger fellow workers are jealous of your relationship with the supervisor. Apparently you are older and perhaps more experienced and therefore more closely identified with the supervisor and more closely associated with him emotionally than the other workers. You can, undoubtedly, lessen the jealousy of the younger workers and thereby contribute to their happiness considerably by trying to become more aware of the many ways in which you could share the supervisor with them and the specific emotional satisfactions you might relinquish in connection with him which would not interfere with your relation with him and which would undoubtedly help the younger workers. You might, in fact, talk to your supervisor about this problem so that he might help you to improve your relations with the younger workers. It is always necessary for us in every situation to share our love with others.

3. Can you suggest ways in which employees can improve their relations with their foremen and the general relations of their groups?

Employees can always improve their relations with their foreman and with their fellow workers through consistently trying to be dependable and reliable and by making daily efforts to understand the other person. Every employee would do well to keep

VIII. *Employer — Employee* [225

in mind that the foreman's position with respect to management and with respect to the employees involves a complex set of relationships and responsibilities that are often difficult and trying. Recognition of this fact will tend to make the workers more tolerant of him and perhaps also more helpful to him. Whatever we can do for others over and above the tasks we are expected to accomplish will invariably be rewarded through increased personal satisfactions. Employees too frequently overlook the importance of giving primary consideration to the needs of others and only secondarily having concern for their own emotional needs.

4. How would it be to have the President and Cabinet of the United States sit once a week with a psychiatrist?

What could be accomplished by such a procedure would depend upon the recognition by the President and the Cabinet that the presence of a psychiatrist during Cabinet meetings might provide opportunity for improving interpersonal relations. Psychiatrists have adequately demonstrated their worth to industrial executives by their presence and the contributions they have been able to make during meetings of executives, but Government itself has not utilized these professional services sufficiently for one to say that any satisfactory results have been accomplished. What has been demonstrated for the top executives of industry, however, could also be demonstrated at the executive level of Government.

5. What part do unions play in employee welfare in the psychiatric field?

As I indicated to you at the beginning, this larger question is beyond my clinical experience and I am therefore not sufficiently well informed to give an adequate answer. The unions have established their own health institutes, and so far as I know, they are rendering satisfactory professional services to employees. The unions have established psychiatric services as part of some of their health institutes, and I imagine they are making every effort to assist employees whenever they can.

6. Might an employer's desire to understand and so forth be interpreted as weakness by an employee and an invitation to take advantage?

If an employer's desire to understand his workers arises from natural motives—that is, if it is a natural expression of his personality—it will never be interpreted as weakness, just as it is never so interpreted in any other series of human relations. We are always grateful when someone else manifests an interest in understanding us, and the same would be true for employees and employers. If, however, an employer's desire to understand his employees is dictated by motives that are not concerned with the happiness and the contentment of the worker, but have for their aim something of gain for the employer himself, they might then well be understood with suspicion and dis-

VIII. *Employer — Employee*

like. We usually know whether someone is genuinely interested in us or is merely pretending to be concerned for our welfare. In some instances we might at first be deceived, but sooner or later we always seem to discern what is genuine and what is artificial.

IX

PASTOR — PARISHIONER

by REV. OTIS R. RICE [1]

WHETHER the pastor is fully aware of it, whether he understands the full implications of it or not, he is dealing with a dynamic of tremendous potential in his relationship with his parishioners. It is scarcely necessary to say that whenever two people come together, a vital dynamic develops. Pastors, like any other professional persons, must recognize this force when dealing with those who seek them out.

In the pastoral relationship the dynamic is probably heightened, because pastor and parishioner are in a peculiar relationship, differing from other professional relationships. It is a privileged one, legally protected, like those of doctor and patient, lawyer and client. No privileged communication to a pastor may be used in court, nor may it be used as evidence. But it is more. An additional bulwark to this relationship is the tradition existing down through the ages that the pastor is one to whom people go with their troubles. A certain authority accrues to the sacred minister because of his ordination and vocation. His position is further heightened and strengthened by the fact that he, unlike other professional persons, may enter a situation without being summoned. Doc-

[1] Religious Director, St. Luke's Hospital, New York.

IX. Pastor — Parishioner

tors and lawyers must, of necessity, be called. But the pastor considers it his duty, within the bounds of tact and discrimination, to enter those situations in which his parishioners are in difficulty. This same relationship also requires that he prepare them for times of remote trouble in which he may serve—a service not usual in the offices of other professional people.

Normally, a pastor occupies a pulpit. He preaches, visits people in various kinds of difficulty, and is an active participant in the epochal events of their lives. He is in a position to prepare them for the normal crises that most parishioners must sometime face. Thus he incurs a special responsibility toward those who come to him saying: "I heard you preach last Sunday. You seemed to be talking to my need. Somehow I feel I can come to you with my troubles."

The pastoral relationship is deepened in this busy age by the fact that the pastor is, in many instances, more available than the psychiatrist or doctor. Psychiatrists, even if available, must make charges that many patients cannot meet. We all know how limited psychiatric resources are at present, even in a great city like New York. Yet the pastor presumably has time available because that is part of his job. Moreover, he is not hampered by such matters as fees and office hours, except in special understandable circumstances.

I grant at once that although the relationship of pastor and parishioner may be strengthened by these considerations, there are those who would *never* think of going to a pastor with *any* problem. It is possible that these people may in the past have consulted a pastor in time of difficulty but have found him a weak, uncomprehending vessel or have been repelled by a rigid attitude of moralism. There is also a tacit distrust of the clergy among many. Nevertheless, within the dynamic of the pastoral relationship there is a potential for good or for ill. We pastors have had our own attitudes toward our parishioners and toward our work greatly affected by studies of other relationships and by insights that come to us from the discipline of psychiatry.

Not for a moment do I imply that we are prepared to practice psychiatry. I do believe, however, that the recognition of the responsibilities and limitations of our relationship is tremendously important for the lives of other people and, of course, for our own. Hence we wish to have our own relationships with others implemented by what has been learned from other disciplines and from experience in other vital relationships. Thus we approach our tasks with a somewhat new attitude. We are actually relearning the things that the great pastors down through the centuries have known. We are beginning to recognize that the dynamic of our relationship is itself much more important than any specific action we may take in the interests of our parishioners.

There are three basic attitudes or assumptions which underlie our pastoral care today. First, the deep and abiding reverence for the integrity of the personality of the parishioner. It may seem curious to mention that the pastor must have reverence for the integrity of the parishioner; but the truth of the matter is that, with the best intentions in the world, pastors have sometimes thought they were doing the Lord's work and will when they made decisions for, gave ad-

IX. *Pastor — Parishioner*

vice to, made plans for, judged, or gave encouragement to others without real warrant.

Today we realize how easy it is for us to violate (even with the best of intentions) the integrity of another. We know that it is far better for an individual to select for his own life a plan that we may believe to be third-rate than for us to try to superimpose on him what we believe to be a first-rate plan. Many times what seems to be common sense is common nonsense. Our advice to a parishioner may actually violate his integrity. For example, a young couple, childless and at swords' points, sought out their pastor. Their difficulties and dissention were such that they had decided to obtain a divorce. The pastor, without understanding their deeper conflicts, said: "What you must do is adopt an infant. The dear little one will bind you together."

Do you sense what happened here? A child so adopted became a battleground upon which two people fought, and in the end the integrity of the child too was violated as well as that of both husband and wife. Ultimately the child became neurotic and the parents separated without any understanding of the emotional factors involved.

In another instance, a pastor was sought out by an avowed alcoholic. The pastor knelt and prayed with his alcoholic parishioner. As they rose from their knees the pastor said: "I am guided by God to urge you to sign a pledge to the Almighty that you will never drink again. I know that God will answer your prayer, because He answers all prayers."

Anyone who has ever dealt with alcoholics knows how dangerous such a procedure can be. But the pledge was signed and the alcoholic left the parsonage. As might have been expected, the desire to drink built up. With unconscious drives impelling him, the alcoholic went off on a three-day spree. When he came to himself and was sober once more, he realized that not only had he failed again, but now he had broken a solemn and absolute pledge to Almighty God. So he hanged himself. Here again was an obvious violation of the integrity of another soul. It is incidents such as these that make malpractice on human souls infinitely more reprehensible than malpractice on human bodies.

To recapitulate, exploitation in the pastoral relationship is a constant danger. Therefore we clergymen are trying to make certain that we develop an intelligent reverence for the integrity of the people we seek to serve.

A second attitude we strive to achieve is a deep and abiding faith in the forces and resources of life. This means that the forces and resources of life are to be trusted. Sometimes these forces and resources are not what the pastor ordinarily has recognized as such. An individual may have great hostility in his heart yet have the potentialities of creativity. Aggression in its many forms may become useful and creative. One of the most horrifying discoveries a pastor can make is that of the aridity in other lives. These disturbed individuals have no responses, no drives, no eagerness in any direction. But the person with plenty of hostility may, in fact, possess potential resources for life and survival. Mistaken loyalties may be turned into creative loyalties; futile fantasies may become constructive imagination. We now believe that within the parishioner himself are forces that can be under-

IX. Pastor — Parishioner

stood and used. We believe that within the situation itself are forces and resources that can be useful and helpful. We affirm that within the pastor-parishioner relationship are forces to be trusted, utilized, and made creative.

We are discovering that it takes time for these forces to be realized. It is not possible to do much for a parishioner in one twenty-minute interview. The discovery of deeper forces may take a considerable length of time. We are learning, also, that many of the drives in the unconscious portions of the mind are not necessarily dirty, infantile, and vicious. One finds there, what is more important, the finer, deeper, more powerful forces that make for integration and real creativity in life.

The informed pastor needs to school himself in a third attitude. It is that of understanding. I use the word in a twofold meaning. The pastor must be willing to be an accepting, permissive individual who at least at the outset of his ministration engages in no condemnation of his parishioner and makes no judgment upon him. He should not be shocked, disgusted, or frightened by the predicament in which he finds his parishioner although the behavior exhibited may be sinful, antisocial, and disgusting. The sacred minister in his pastoral role must be willing to make himself available for the needs of others. He is also understanding in a second sense: he seeks to discover the *meaning* of the parishioner's problem or behavior. Again and again the pastor must ask himself: "What does this behavior mean for this parishioner at this time?" Or "What is my parishioner's *feeling* in this situation which has come to my attention?"

It is difficult but necessary for the pastor to remember that the same external pattern of behavior may have quite different meanings for different individuals and for the same person under varying circumstances. Such an antisocial act as stealing or lying may be reprehensible and immoral. But the pastor's primary concern is to discover *why* an individual lies or steals, what the emotional and spiritual significance of the act is to those concerned. The understanding of behavior is difficult even for those adept in psychiatry and psychology; but it is a necessary attitude and attribute of the pastor who deals with human souls.

I have used three words: *reverence, faith,* and *understanding*. We pastors are quite familiar with their general meaning, yet we must add a new meaning to them: *reverence* for the integrity of the individual, *faith* in the forces of life, and *understanding* of the individual's predicament. Putting these three principles into operation means, of course, that most of us in our pastor-parishioner relationships must become *listeners* and *observers*. Here it is the relationship itself that has meaning. Instead of presenting an immediate and final answer for our parishioner, we must listen—listen to discover his real problem, listen to discern our own reaction to his behavior.

Someone has said that good pastoral care is *trained listening*. Well, you know, for a clergyman listening is the hardest thing in the world to do. After all, we are trained to preach or pray at the drop of a hat! To listen is a tremendous sacrifice! But it is a sacrifice we must make if we really love people. We must be willing to sit back and listen to their problems. The dynamic of

IX. *Pastor — Parishioner*

the relationship itself does something in respect to the predicament of our parishioner.

Pastors have a remarkable gamut of normal relations with people at critical times in their lives. When a baby is born, arrangements are made for baptism, dedication, or circumcision. The impact of the pastor upon the family and the godparents is felt, and a relationship set up. This relationship may have deep meaning later on in the life of the growing child, and his family as well.

In the period of early childhood we are concerned with the religious education of the child within the family circle. We are also concerned with the community in which the family lives and in which the child develops.

At adolescence we encounter our young people as we prepare them for confirmation or full membership in the Church. Confirmation instruction is ordinarily allotted to the pastor. Thus an intimate relationship is set up between these youths and himself. Confirmation instruction is often given individually by the wise pastor so that in this relationship, at a critical point in growth, he may make his influence creative.

Marriage usually is the next opportunity. The pastor gives premarital instruction at another normal crisis of life and officiates at a ceremony of great significance to the couple and the community alike.

Later, in illness or accident, the pastor as a matter of course seeks out his parishioners. In old age (a much more important problem now for the pastor than ever before) there is further opportunity for the relationship. The precepts that have applied before apply with particular cogency to this phase of ministry.

There are, too, the normal crises of death and bereavement. Everyone dies. This is a normal part of life. The pastor has his special function at the time of death. His is also an important role in serving the bereaved persons when death has occurred.

Now, each one of these nodal points in the developmental life of the individual offers the pastor the opportunity to use creatively the relationship existing, or susceptible of being created, between himself and his parishioner. Each of these situations permits him to build up a kind of remote preparation for further ministry in later crises.

Those of us who have ministered for some years in the same community look back with great satisfaction upon the baptism of a child, his introduction into the church school, his preparation for confirmation, his instruction for marriage, and the solemnization of his marriage. This continuity of relationship means, or should mean, that anyone in special difficulty may seek out his pastor and discuss his difficulties with an understanding, reverent person whom he has known in other situations and in other crises. This specialized pastoral relationship today is called pastoral counseling. Pastoral counseling, however, is only one aspect of the pastor-parishioner relationship.

Pastoral counseling today is not very different from what it has been in the hands of informed and loving pastors down through the ages. It is usually well informed by the disciplines of psychiatry, sociology, and anthropology. I hope that we pastors today know our limitations. I trust that we know we are not psychiatrists nor psychiatric social workers nor physicians. Our field is a limited one. Yet within our limitations

IX. Pastor — Parishioner

there is something very real and very much our own to contribute. There is growing up a body of experience and understanding through this special ministry.

We differ among ourselves as to precisely what constitutes pastoral counseling. We do know that it is an extension of the trained listening process and the willingness of the pastor to be available to his people. His parishioner is permitted to present his problem, to marshal his own resources for solving that problem. He then tries for a solution. But he must always be welcome to return with his failures, his successes, and what insights he has gained from trying out a plan discovered and decided upon by the pastor and the parishioner in consultation.

The choice is always to be made—or almost always—by the parishioner himself. The pastor simply allows himself to be used in the relationship so that resources may become apparent and usable, so that new horizons may appear for the parishioner.

The problems are often very simple. The parishioner comes to talk to the pastor about his difficulties. A rapport is thus built which in itself may be enough. The ventilation of simple emotional problems, the catharsis that comes from bringing difficulties out into the open, may be all that is necessary. As we all know, there is all the difference in the world between rumination upon one's own problems and discussing them freely with someone who can be trusted to understand.

The other day a young woman came to talk about which of two men she should marry. By the time she had talked at length about each of these men, she became quite certain that she would marry neither of them! She realized then that she was not ready for marriage and that there were "plenty of other fish in the sea." She had solved her problem by simply talking it out.

Again and again a parishioner may return to the pastor. He may talk for half an hour or an hour at each visit. The pastor says nothing at all. But at the end of the talk the parishioner may go away saying: "Thank you very much. You've been extremely helpful. It's wonderful what you are able to do for your people!"

This is good counseling. The more of this type of listening that can be done, the better. As I said before, we pastors are frequently inclined to talk too much. The encouraging grunt, the quiet, simple word of understanding, is much more helpful than any lecture or the repetition of purple passages from last Sunday's sermon.

Pastoral counseling does involve trained, understanding listening. It is in the listening process that help comes. Listening to catch various "danger signals" may tell the pastor that he cannot deal with the problem. It must be referred to someone specially equipped to handle it. There are the danger signals of serious emotional or mental disturbance that may actually become acute and dangerous if the parishioner is permitted to talk too much. Some people, as they talk, become more and more excited, and more and more unconscious material comes close to the threshold of consciousness. If it breaks through, the parishioner may become seriously ill and have to be hospitalized. These symptoms and danger signals we must learn to recognize.

The art of referral is a matter for serious considera-

IX. Pastor — Parishioner

tion. It is extremely difficult for the pastor to know how to refer to another agency, or to some psychiatric resource, even when it exists. It is often a very delicate task. In these days, too, as I have intimated, it is difficult to find the needed resources. The pastor must sometimes weigh in his own mind whether, lacking other resources, he should himself continue in the situation, doing the best he can without other help. This is one of the ethical problems that every pastor meets as he counsels with his people.

In all his work he uses the same three basic assumptions and principles I have mentioned. He constantly examines his own heart to see whether he is in any way violating the integrity of the person who is entrusted to his care. He seeks to discover the resources within the situation. He must try again and again to understand what is happening, to understand not only what the parishioner believes to be the problem but that deeper problem which underlies the one presented.

In this pastoral-counseling procedure there are rewarding results. Yet if its forces are not understood and carefully used, the relationship can easily get out of hand. If the pastor becomes irritated and hostile, or too emotionally identified with his parishioner, he is likely to abrogate the whole relationship.

No pastor can be completely objective in every instance. He is a human being. His own feelings can become involved. A friend of mine, a very good psychiatrist in this city, said: "One in about every fifty patients makes me so mad that I kick him right out of the office and down the corridor." He continued: "While that loses me one patient, it is good for the other forty-nine!" I suspect that it is more difficult for pastors to kick their parishioners about than it is for a psychiatrist, but nevertheless the human reaction of hostility does enter the situation!

We pastors also recognize, I think, that involvement with others, both positively and negatively, is felt in our own attitude toward them. We should be suspicious when we become drowsy during a pastoral-counseling period, or when we find ourselves sitting on the edge of the chair, only too eager to hear the next naughty revelation! Either one of these attitudes is unproductive. For it shows that we are not trying to help.

Many of the clergy who do pastoral counseling have no business to do so. There are others, however, who are now well trained indeed, and who can supplement other resources in the community. Usually they do a better job with their own parishioners because they share with them a common background.

The pastor also has certain definite resources not always vouchsafed to other professional people. There are the resources of the worshipping, working, and studying congregation. He is the leader of a congregation or a fellowship into which may be introduced the individual with whom he is working. In common worship, common work, and common study there is a togetherness that is very much needed in our culture.

We know only too well how lonely some people are today, and how much of the aridity of life springs from the fact that there is no easy give-and-take in social situations. New York City, despite its rich offerings, is one of the loneliest places in the world. People can be lost among the multitude and no one seems to care.

There are also some specific religious resources. One of them is the Word of God. Holy Writ contains

IX. Pastor — Parishioner

many useful elements as it is read by or expounded to the individual. It can be used in many interesting ways.

In the hospital where I serve, patients tell me that when I read the "Begats" or the Psalms in my usual monotonous voice it is an extremely good sedative! I am not insulted or disturbed when I find that a patient goes to sleep while I am reading. I feel this may be quite therapeutic. The Word of God can be used in other ways, and each individual may use it in a different form.

One should mention the art and power of prayer. Not prayer as an escape from life, but prayer as a means of tapping resources outside the individual and to give him a peace of mind and a sense of relatedness to others and to God which he might not otherwise have.

Theology, not a popular subject today, also is a resource for the pastor. Theology answers, with the authority of the centuries of the Church behind it, many of the most terrifying questions in the world. Unmerited suffering, the problem of evil, and the question of injustice in the world—these are some of the questions for which theology has time-tested answers.

In the use of rites, sacraments, and sacramentals are real resources. We may differ among ourselves on precisely what these are. Yet each religious heritage has some ordinances that may be extremely useful adjuncts to the pastoral relationship.

The fellowship of the Church, the common tradition, worship before a common altar, and the recognition of common sins and common problems are aids to growth and integration. So in that fellowship one feels that one is not alone; one *belongs*, as a cadet in the great tradition of a great house. Therefore one need not feel the loss of integrity or that one has ceased to be a *person*. With these common resources an individual comes close to others who hold the same values and strive for the same goals.

The pastor is a preacher. There is a kind of counseling and a pastor-parishioner relationship that can be achieved from the pulpit. I would not go so far as to say that preaching is group therapy, but preaching certainly can be the introduction to a kind of group therapy and an introduction to the individual-pastoral relationship. The pastor as a local leader has something to say about community standards and community activity.

You will be interested, I think, to know what is being done in the training of pastors for assuming the kind of relationship I have been discussing. Some pastors are "naturals" in this respect. Because of deep natural insights and understanding they are capable of creative pastor-parishioner relationships without the usual trouble or danger. They have had no formal clinical training. Most of us, however, feel that we must be trained and disciplined in our work with others. So we seek to find out something about ourselves. If psychiatrists need to be counseled and analyzed, then certainly the pastor who is to deal with the deepest spiritual and emotional problems needs himself to be counseled. Certainly no confessor would think of hearing a confession unless he were himself making adequate and frequent use of the sacrament of penance. The clergymen of today are seeking counsel in order that they in turn may counsel others.

IX. *Pastor — Parishioner*

Many of the clergy are being tested by various projective tests such as the Rorschach analysis in order to discover their own unused resources, their hidden conflicts, and the means by which they can achieve greater emotional efficiency and freedom. There is an especially valuable asset in clinical pastoral experience under guidance. The Council for Clinical Training, Inc., for example, is devoted exclusively to the training of seminarians and clergy of all faiths.

It all comes back to the clergyman himself. Health begets health. If the pastor is spiritually and psychologically healthy his relationships with others will be health-inspiring and health-creating. But many of us perpetuate pathology because we ourselves are emotionally and spiritually ill. If we cannot healthily relate ourselves to other people, we cannot possibly deal wisely with the personal problems of others. A pastor's ability in the pastor-parishioner relationship depends in large measure upon his own maturity, his own adjustment, the kind of religion he has espoused and the kind of rich-mindedness and understanding he himself possesses.

I have talked much about *relationship,* but I have really been talking about religion, because religion is a matter of relationship. It is a question of how one relates to himself, to others, and to God. Religion is inherent in every relationship whether one is technically religious or not. Certainly there are many times when the relationship speaks for itself and we need not use the more formal symbols of religion. We parsons need to pray before we undertake relationships with other people, but we do not necessarily use formal prayer in our counseling sessions. The quality of our relationship with ourselves, with other people, and with God is a religious matter whether formally so understood or not.

1. Do you think that every couple of whatever age should seek pastoral counseling before seeking divorce, even though they are not church members?

That depends a good deal on the skill of the pastor to be consulted, and also on the couple's purpose in seeking counsel. If they are entirely outside any religious tradition and if the pastor is not adept in marital counseling, there would be little to be gained. Marital counseling is one of the most difficult tasks for the psychiatrist or pastoral counselor, and unless the individuals concerned are genuinely eager to have some help, not much can be accomplished.

Regarding church membership and pastoral counseling, one should remember that there are many clergymen of all faiths who make themselves available to those who are not members of their own congregation or fellowship. It is always difficult, of course, to discover which pastors are trained or skilled in counseling. Usually the experience of other persons who have been successfully counseled will be a good guide.

2. Must certain prescribed psychiatric courses be taken by a pastor before he can undertake to do work as a pastoral counselor?

Any pastor can do pastoral counseling whether he has had special training experience or not.

IX. Pastor — Parishioner

It is unfortunate that many of the clergy do undertake a form of counseling in which they are not properly skilled. An increasingly large number of the clergy, however, are receiving special training and instruction in the important field of personal counseling. Some also take a prescribed course leading to a doctorate in philosophy, so that their competence is comparable to that of licensed psychologists.

3. What about the person who attends church frequently but because he is not particularly aggressive is not looked up or called on? Many times he needs and wishes the help of a pastor more than the others.

It is always a difficult question for the pastor whether he will seem to be intruding if he goes out of his way to speak to a parishioner or to call on him, or whether he should simply make it known to the members of his congregation that he is always available and eager to discuss problems with them. Some clergy have the happy faculty of approaching people in such a way that they are neither annoyed nor embarrassed. It is my own view that the clergy need constantly to call upon their parishioners in their own homes so that they may be familiar with family situations and individual needs. If it is their custom to make such regular visits on members of their congregation, there will be ample opportunity for persons in need of help to indicate their desire and to present their problems.

4. When you feel that psychiatry will help a parishioner, do you find it difficult to advise it? People so often still feel they do not need it.

One of the most difficult functions of pastoral counseling is to help the individual to a realization that he needs psychiatric assistance. It is often possible for the individual to recognize for himself the need for psychotherapy, and when the rapport between parishioner and clergyman is strong, the pastor can refer him to a psychiatric colleague.

5. How can a person tell whether a particular pastor is qualified to counsel him?

There is no certain means for ascertaining the skill or qualifications of a clergyman for pastoral counseling. Ministers who have had formal clinical training under such auspices as the Council for Clinical Training Inc. of New York or the Institute of Pastoral Care in Boston are usually competent in this field.

A gauge of a pastor's qualifications is the kind of understanding sermons he preaches and the quality of his general pastoral ministrations.

6. Is psychiatry included in a clergyman's education?

Psychiatric training as such is not included in the clergyman's education, but seminarians in many seminaries are being trained in pastoral psychology, which is an introduction to the type of trained ministry I have been talking about. A few clergy are

IX. Pastor — Parishioner

trained as *psychiatrists*, but they go through the usual medical and psychiatric training *in addition* to their theological studies.

A clergyman is not a psychiatrist but a professional person in his own right. He therefore does not need full medical and psychiatric training, but surely does need some of the insights deriving from the disciplines of medicine and psychiatry.

Several seminaries require a period of clinical training in addition to the regular curriculum, and many seminarians in other divinity schools themselves elect the training because of their own felt need. I have mentioned the Council for Clinical Training Inc., which trains men at twenty centers—general hospitals, mental hospitals and prisons—for the better performance of the pastoral ministry. At these centers the students not only receive insights from other disciplines which may be useful in their own proper sphere, but under *theological* supervision gain experience in dealing with the actual spiritual and emotional problems of persons in difficulty.

7. **Do you advocate psychoanalysis for the pastor? And I mean actual psychoanalysis, not occasional counseling.**

Many clergymen and seminarians would profit greatly from psychoanalysis. It would implement their understanding of themselves, their pastoral relationships, and the behavior of their parishioners. The need for analysis for the clergy is somewhat parallel to the like need on the part of social workers and physicians. Pastors whose own neurotic problems interfere with their effectiveness might be good candidates for psychoanalytic therapy. At the present it would be quite impossible to make psychoanalysis a requirement of the preparation for the sacred ministry, even if desirable.

X

CITIZEN — COMMUNITY

by GEORGE S. STEVENSON, M.D.[1]

It is not difficult to find interesting and significant episodes reflecting the psychological side of citizen-community relationships. Some time ago a young citizen of the United States, impelled by a praiseworthy concern over the international situation, renounced his citizenship. He did this to become what he called "a citizen of the world." He thereupon set himself up with headquarters in Paris to serve as a pattern and to encourage others similarly to enter upon world citizenship.

About a year later, while in Amsterdam, I was approached by a newspaper reporter who wanted to get my opinion of this whole affair. To renounce the citizenship of any other country would not cause so much excitement, but American citizenship is usually rated high, and to relinquish it is to make news.

It seemed to be a new idea to this reporter that one would be unable, in fact, to become a world citizen merely by relinquishing one's responsibility to one's country, state, and locality. I had to set forth rather strongly that in order to become a world citizen, one needed first to succeed in one's relationship with the

[1] Johns Hopkins. Medical Director of the National Association for Mental Health; past president, American Psychiatric Association.

people close about one, in one's family and neighborhood. All the people of the world live in families and in neighborhoods, and there alone can they develop the solid foundation in human relations that is essential for citizenship at any level, especially at the level of the most complex of all communities, the world.

One thing we all have in common is that we live in local communities. It is there that people rise on their successes or fall under their failures. What happens throughout the state, nation, or world is important only as it affects these lives, these successes, and these failures. The plans and accomplishments of those individuals working in broader areas are validated only by what happens to people at home. In so far as good citizen-community relations become the basis for what is done, the good is multiplied and promulgated over a larger territory. The same is true of bad relations. In brief, international amity does not begin in Geneva or in the United Nations or in any other world center. It begins at home. Geneva is where it is developed for world application.

Some time ago I attended a conference in Cleveland called by the United States National Commission of the United Nations Educational, Scientific, and Cultural Organization (UNESCO). UNESCO is the keystone in our growing world structure. Its purpose is to develop a world opinion, a world attitude that will cause the people of every country in the world to want to take part in and to be citizens and not subjects of such a world government as is needed. It is the task of the National Commission to develop this attitude here in the United States. This task is most difficult. The greatest barrier that confronts those working toward

X. Citizen — Community [251]

this goal is the hostility of people to difference. People are hostile to the difference in the way things are, and are done, in other countries. They are often hostile to difference in various parts of their own country or even other parts of their own neighborhood. The obstacle is our inability to be comfortable in the face of such difference. It is still harder to find positive values in difference, or pleasure and satisfaction in difference.

The great task of UNESCO is to overcome these obstacles, to help people to be comfortable, to find positive value and to get pleasure and satisfaction out of the fact that the human animal is so flexible and so richly endowed that he can solve life's problems in different ways according to environmental conditions. Over the world the basic needs of people are pretty much alike; but the means employed to meet these needs are infinitely diverse. We here in the United States have our public-health services; a South Sea Islander may build his house on poles. His family status may be reflected in the collection of heads passed down by his ancestors from cutthroat warfare; we have our social register, derived from a more figurative cutthroat competition. If we in this way can focus on the common needs and can recognize the similar strivings of all people, we can with less discomfort and less hostility understand and accept the very different conditions under which these needs may be met.

This UNESCO conference to which I referred was seeking ways in which this could be accomplished. Thousands of people attended, full of earnestness, anxious that this endeavor should be successful and anxious to do their bit. Anxiety is a great driving force, and if the effort is directed toward the amelioration of our condition, we make progress. But anxiety is in turn allayed by our doing something, so that the something that is done must be effective, otherwise the incentive is removed without gain. The importance of the thing done ought to be taken into account in judging the suggestions that are brought forth in such a conference: are they gestures or do they really help to transcend the barriers of these attitudes toward difference that hamper our international growth?

One of the frequently suggested techniques for overcoming these barriers is the verbal appeal, exhortation. Another is the pageant. Both are of doubtful value. A very common example of the latter type is the classroom pageant in which children are dressed up in foreign costumes, perhaps performing the characteristic dances or showing other typical customs of a national group. It is assumed that such displays will improve the attitude of actors and audience toward the people so portrayed. The point is missed that such passive, superficial experiences do not affect attitudes. One can witness these pageants, look upon them as quaint or exotic, learn something new about the dress or customs of another group, but come away with little if any change of attitude. On the other hand, in every classroom every day there are very concrete experiences that offer opportunities to modify attitudes toward difference. Things are happening that are personal and have emotional significance to those involved and so are closely tied in with attitudes. When one teacher works out methods of dealing with these day-by-day opportunities, she can pass them on to fellow teachers elsewhere through the second, third, and fourth stories of our structure.

X. Citizen — Community

I think of a most conscientious rural teacher who wanted to do the right thing. She had her pageants. She also had, but failed to use constructively, more humble but promising ways of affecting attitudes toward difference. Helen, one of her pupils, had come from a distant state where they do not say *wåter* with a broad *a*, but *wăter*, with a short one. Here was a clear opportunity for this teacher to show what a monotonous world this would be if everybody followed the same patterns. She could have shown that Helen is right when she says *wăter* and the other pupils are right, too, when they say *wåter*. Instead she attempted to press Helen into saying *wåter*. Without such pressure Helen probably would soon have been using the same pronunciation as the other children, but instead she resisted this intrusion and lack of respect for her personality and stuck to her family pattern. Not only that, but the whole class was given an example of intolerance, and their chances of entering the second, third, and fourth stories of citizenship were blocked. Helen was made allergic to the customs and differences of her adopted community. She finally expressed her hostility by asking the teacher: "How do you spell *idear*?" for the teacher's pronunciation included a final *r* sound on this word.

I have used the teacher merely as an example, although a most important one. The teacher is anxiously and earnestly looking for ways of doing something about this world of ours. No group is striving more sincerely, yet no one has given her the kind of help that she needs. Her training has not given her enough basic understanding of how attitudes are changed. It has given her too much emphasis on the principle that there is only one right way and that all others are wrong ways. Anxious to do her part, she is receptive to suggestions. She needs help to evaluate these suggestions, help to enable her to recognize and to utilize creatively the myriad opportunities for broadening attitudes presented in the day-by-day life in each classroom community. That would make for sounder construction on the first-story level of citizenship.

How can the citizen come to understand his community and begin to relate himself effectively to it? There are several ways. He might list all of the different divisions of community function—that is, might look into all of the community agencies to see what is there and what they mean. But to understand the schools, the police, health, and welfare agencies of a modern metropolis presents such a stupendous task that he would soon become bogged down and discouraged. When he got through, there is a good chance that in his understanding these would still be separate agencies rather than parts of an integrated community.

On the other hand, he might pick out some special interest such as mental health. If he followed this interest through its various ramifications in the community, he would find himself following a thread that would lead him to practically all of the agencies and would at the same time relate them to each other and to him as a citizen.

The reason for this is simple. After all, a community's services reflect the needs of its people. In each person these needs exist as an integrated whole. There is no such thing as their being isolated. There is no exclusively ailing or praying or playing person. Thus if

X. Citizen — Community

one pursues any one of these aspects in a person he is led to the whole living of that person, and if he pursues any one phase of community service he is similarly led to every community service. A study of mental health in the community leads him through the needs, the strivings and disappointments of its people, and in that way he can discover the deficiencies in other fields such as education or recreation, even though technically they are outside of the health field. Anyone who extends his interest in the direction of prevention, by the same token is led into a number of other fields, for seldom are the causes of a problem to be found in the same field as the problem itself. The community services are thus a kind of mosaic picture of a functioning man. Some of the stones depict education, some religion, some medical service, and some recreation. But as a community exists today, many of these stones are out of place or missing, and thus fail to depict a community that is truly representative of its people and its needs.

When the citizen has come to understand his community in terms of people and their problems and needs, an interesting thing happens. He very quickly takes a second step and says to himself: "What is behind these problems? What is behind sickness, illiteracy, school failure, delinquency, family dissolution, and poverty?" He discovers that the hidden world behind all these problems is not different for each but the same for all. So if he tries to define preventive work for each of the fields, he finds that for the school, the court, the police, the doctor, and others it is always the same. He is back among the things that affect mental health and influence human behavior. These are no longer psychiatry, or education, or public health alone; they are all of them. They are the subsoil for all, but the exclusive realm of none. He may even find the leaders in the various agencies sometimes quarreling over proprietary responsibility for preventive work. He will certainly find again and again several forces that are basic in citizen-community problems. Our inquiring citizen could keep an index card for each of these forces, note their occurrence, and highlight their importance.

One such card might be headed "Inhumanity." This would not mean outright cruelty so much as neglect. He would find that today we are less moved by human need and misery than we used to be. We are less personal and more detached. The simplest way of dealing with a problem used to be to lend a neighborly hand out of compassion, but this often led to abuses. For example, children were often exploited by their foster parents, so the local government stepped in and took over the responsibility for placing wards. From old records we learn that often the county determined how much it would pay by auctioning off the ward to the lowest bidder. A farmer might offer to care for a homeless child for two dollars a month; another would agree to take responsibility for a mentally deficient man for a dollar and a half a month.

While the assumption of control by the county provided some safeguard against the abuses, it also removed the element of compassion. This was eliminated almost completely when the county decided to go into the guardianship business itself. It set up almshouses, but being a governmental department rather than a person, it could not inject the element of com-

X. Citizen — Community

passion. Probably the extremes of cruelty became fewer and the controls stronger, but certainly humanity was replaced by routine. Many such almshouses had herded within their walls the old, the blind, the orphaned, the mentally defective, and the mentally sick with no provision for their different specific needs.

When Dorothea Dix one hundred years ago initiated a drive to replace the almshouses by state asylums for the mentally ill, there was no compassion left to lose and there was a great deal to gain technically by the change. The state had more resources, and the concentration of effort permitted better technical service. But just as compassion had slipped out of the picture without our appreciating what was happening, so with the establishment of state asylums mentally ill persons were taken farther and farther away from the grass roots where the causes of their problems lay and where they had to fit in again upon their recovery. The distance of a state hospital from the community of its patients in some states today is as much as six hundred miles. There was an assumption that recovery could be achieved within the walls of the institution. New York in recent legislation has shown its recognition that this is not recovery but merely the beginning of convalescence, and that convalescence must be continued back in the community if it is to be effective. Prior to this change a patient leaving a mental hospital was described as "on parole," as though he were discharged upon his promise of good behavior. He is now more realistically said to be "on convalescent care."

The detachment from the near neighbor to the far neighbor, to the almshouse, and then to the state asylum is what I mean by progressive inhumanity. Maybe *un*humanity is a better word. In any case, humanity is suppressed.

I wish I could say how this element of humanity can be retrieved. I do not believe we want to give up the technical advances we have made in order to keep people in the home town. I know there are many possible ties to the home and to the community that are now left slack. I mean such things as social work, clinics, volunteers, community consultation, and vocational rehabilitation for patients, co-operative relationships with medical schools in both research and training, and open house for the public. Utilizing these ties will not induce compassion but will tend to minimize the isolation of the hospital patient's plight. In any case, if we only recognize that compassion has passed out of the picture we shall no longer depend upon it to ensure the proper quality of service and will be prepared to search for an impelling substitute if we are citizens concerned with our communities and the problems of people living in them. So much for the card headed "Inhumanity."

Our second card might be headed "Disintegration." It may seem paradoxical to say that community functions have disintegrated in this age when they have reached their highest technical level, but please recognize that community functions are today sharply categorized and departmentalized. People become "criminals," or "invalids," or "indigents," or "illiterates," or "unemployed," or "spiritually bewildered." Seldom are they just *people* with any or all of these problems. If a person gets into a categorical channel he gets excel-

X. *Citizen — Community* [259

lent help within that channel, but it is hard to get into other channels of help also. Therein lies the disintegration.

An integer is a whole number as opposed to a fraction. Disintegration means fractionation, which is our present state. The wholeness of service to the person in his community is gone. Only the small rural community retains a remnant of integration. There generalized functionaries still exist. You will see a rural schoolteacher doing a well-rounded job because she lives in a less complex community, knows the important things about its families, can take all of these small but pertinent factors into account in dealing with a child in her classroom, and secures help effectively from other technical community resources because she knows them and how they work.

New York presents a glaring example of disintegration. It will require more than good intentions and the best leadership in a welfare council to pull the hundreds of its community agencies into an integrated whole. Walk into the headquarters of the different city departments and look at their district maps. The police, health, schools, and other departments are all districted so differently that if the citizens in a neighborhood want to bring about joint action by these agencies, they find themselves blocked by very different geographical divisions of responsibility.

So it is in most large communities. Our agencies are comparable to a large number and variety of fine musical instruments. We have expert artists playing them, but they are all playing solos and we have no orchestra. The professions, too, tend to perpetuate this departmentalization. It is the citizen in his relationship to the community who can combat this wholesale violation of mental health.

Our interested citizen, following further the mental hygiene thread through his complex community, is told that about one in every one hundred and fifty of his fellow citizens has serious mental illness to such a degree that a court has said he is legally insane. He will see occasionally a seriously disturbed person in the street, but in no such ratio as that. He does not see his community hospitals housing these patients, nor do his neighbors tell him about the breakdowns in their families. He discovers that mental hospitals are hidden far away, that people don't talk about their insane relatives, and that this fosters another vicious aspect of disintegration—the isolation of the hospitals and the subsequent isolation of their patients.

Service deteriorates because facilities are inadequate and staff is hard to secure. Not many are willing to live and work out of contact with the community and with centers of professional stimulation even though the pay is good. In many hospitals the pay is not sufficiently high. Families lose contact and find new familial adjustments without the sick member. The patients in general hospitals stay in their communities or in near-by communities. Their families visit them, they offer sympathy and respect such as a sick person deserves; but in the mental hospital they do not.

Many hospitals have three beds in a space built for two, and under these conditions indecent things happen. But even more the kitchens, the laundries, the water supply, and the power are overtaxed and serve poorly because they were not planned for a fifty-per-

X. Citizen — Community   [261

cent overload. Staff quarters, also, are too scant, and nurses, attendants, and operating staff suffer inconvenience. With this added to their recreational and social limitations, staff members become discontented or resign. All of this is bad for the patient.

The clothing of the patient is poor. One would not think of wearing it in everyday life. In fact, sometimes the clothing does not even exist. So much for clothing.

At home people also expect protection of life and limb. We have police to serve that purpose. It is part of modern decent living, but in our mental hospitals where there are shortages or inadequacies of personnel no such protection is afforded. In fact, brutality under state auspices is far too frequent. Citizens in communities can readily appreciate these contradictory roles of the state.

As the citizen studies the life of the patient in the mental hospital, comparing it with what the average member of the community demands as a decent standard of living, he encounters deficiency upon deficiency. Not only do housing, clothing, and protection fail to meet the test; food, opportunity to work, maintenance of family ties, accordance of respect and recreation are all below standard. He discovers that these things exist because the thread is so thin between the hospital and the community that it assures no effective connection—only isolation.

Thinking about his card headed "Isolation," the citizen would find it closely tied up with two others: "Economy" and "Administrative Expediency."

Usually hospitals are geographically isolated from their communities because land is cheaper out of the cities and towns. In early days, too, this represented economy on another basis: each hospital cut its costs by having its own farm. Then, legislatures do not make adequate appropriations. Why? Is it that legislators don't want to, or is it because they feel that the citizens expect them to curtail tax levies by such corner-cutting? It is almost always the latter. If legislators know from their constituents that they believe "economy" of this type dangerous, that they don't want it, they will appropriate more adequately for this budget item.

The element of economy is always a misleading one. After all, were we operating primarily by the economy yardstick we could ape Hitler's ways of doing so—more ways than any of us would care to think about. We could remove the barriers to suicide; that would eliminate some patients, and that would be cheaper. We could remove the segregation of the active tuberculous cases; then this disease could spread more rapidly and produce more deaths, and the number of patients would be smaller. But why enumerate more? Economy can't be our primary criterion.

Perhaps "Administrative Expediency" is inevitably hand in glove with "Isolation." I'm not sure, but it is evidently much easier to run a hospital if you are not bothered by having too frequent contacts with the community—if you welcome a patient at the door and say good-by to him as a convalescent when he leaves. Ramifications out into the community such as social workers, clinics, family care of patients in private homes, research connections with medical schools, and vocational rehabilitation for patients who need redirection in a healthier job are always administratively complicated. Very complicated and inexpedient is an

X. Citizen — Community

arrangement they have in a hospital that serves Detroit. There they require that each of the doctors on the staff go out and be a doctor in the community as well, and his patients remain his patients in the hospital. But they are not gathered in two or three wards; they are scattered throughout the wards, depending upon where they belong in the hospital's classification of its patients. This is administratively inexpedient and inconvenient, but it and things like it are important to the goal of really serving sick people.

The thoughtfully investigative citizen might find labels for several more cards in his study of the underlying causes of the inadequacy of hospital care of the mentally ill. But repeatedly he would find that each cause can be influenced by more actively responsible citizen-community relations. Our sick have what we citizens want them to have or permit them to have.

The psychotic patients in mental hospitals, however, are but one segment of the citizens upon whose lives mental illness has cast a blight. A far larger group, neurotics, are walking around in their communities. Often they are not recognized as mentally ill. Often their problem is one of disturbance within only a narrow sphere; but it frequently, for the individual sufferer, disables him as completely as if he were ill enough to be in a hospital. Recognized or not, these ills which so seriously cripple the lives of neurotic individuals and their family groups exist in communities that have woefully inadequate facilities for providing help.

In following our mental-hygiene thread we find that every one of these sick people, whether a psychotic in a hospital or a psychoneurotic treated in an outside clinic, points to factors in the community that failed him before he received treatment. His history points to them, his symptoms point to them, his family points to them. These factors in the community are too numerous for us to discuss all of them. But looking briefly at a few might be provocative of later more careful and adequate consideration.

These mental sicknesses point back to the family physician. It is part of the job of every doctor to recognize that his patients often talk to him in riddles. They don't come straight to the point sometimes because they are afraid to face what they suspect may be really wrong with them—cancer, heart disease, tuberculosis. Sometimes they feel rather vaguely that their ill health is tied up with their attitudes, their current life experiences, or their habits, but this feeling may be too vague to express or too painful to face. Sometimes the difficulty is caused by the taboos still surrounding mental and emotional disorders, and patient and doctor beat about the bush calling the trouble "nervousness," as if it were caused by something physiologically wrong with the nerves.

The physician must be able skillfully to bring the patient to the point where he can talk about these feared or tabooed aspects of his health problem; then he must be equipped to help the total man who sits across the desk. Two outstanding barriers have stood in the way of such attainments, both in the nature of educational deficits.

The general idea which has been developed about illness is that it is caused by some organ or body tissue —a kidney, a lung, a heart—that shows some abnormality which can be diagnosed under a microscope or

X. Citizen — Community

by other laboratory techniques and then treated by pills or injections or surgery. There is much talk about behavior, but it is of a heart or a lung whose behavior is out of line, not of a whole human being who is out of line. To be given an opportunity to sit down and have a two-way talk about the whole man whose individual organ seems to be giving trouble is usually a shock and surprise to a patient. He ordinarily hasn't thought of that as a doctor's job. Expansion of public education along the lines of what we know of the psychosomatic realities of illness will help lower this barrier.

The second barrier has been in the physician's educational preparation for helping patients. Until recently the general practitioner has for the most part been dependent upon intuition, chance, or at best the unconscious copying of a master of this art with whom as a young doctor he has been associated. It has not been a regular part of his medical school's curriculum. Particularly since the war, during which medical men encountered so many problems of this nature, the returning M.D.'s have been demanding supplementary training in psychiatry, and medical schools are evolving a more realistic curriculum.

Many patients point back to their relations with their clergymen. Sometimes what they have received from them has been extremely valuable and they have broken down in spite of it; sometimes it has been relatively without value; sometimes it has even raised quandaries that have complicated their problems further. We have often failed to distinguish between guilt that is justified and neurotic feelings of guilt that are not tied to significant misdeeds. Such generalized guilt feelings have roots a long way back in the individual's life.

Then the patient points back to industry, to his job, to his absences from it, to the days when he did not produce very much in it. Those who were supervising him did not see that these events were expressions of illness. Management often did little to preserve a rather expensive investment that it had made in the training of the individual worker. There is some improvement now, but much remains to be done.

It is interesting that back in 1943 we put on a drive to broaden the scope of the Federal Vocational Rehabilitation Act so that it could include the mentally handicapped. Up to that time vocational handicaps were not supposed to ensue from mental disabilities. The amended act made it possible for a state to get fifty per cent of the cost of vocational training from the Federal Government, and one hundred per cent of the cost of supervising the training program; and yet by 1946 I think Michigan was the only state that was doing very much with it.

The patient also points back to the court. Many of those in hospitals have been through court proceedings. Some of these court proceedings are so hidden, so informal, that the patient isn't much aware—actually in many places isn't aware at all—that the court is involved. The court reviews all of the commitment papers, but does not call the patient before it.

In Texas a patient is still accused, in a formal court setting. The judge says: "You are charged with being insane. How do you plead?" The patient enters a plea of not guilty. A plea of guilty is not accepted. The trial is then held. The jury of six retires and comes back

X. Citizen — Community

with a judgment that this man is guilty of insanity. So the patient in Texas is much more likely to point to the court than one in New York, or in New Jersey, where the damage done by the court is less significant.

But quite apart from the commitment procedure, many of these patients come up before the court in the early stages of their problems with behavior difficulties or crimes that are not recognized as symbols of mental disorder, and so they point back to the history of a period in which they served a sentence.

Again, many are taken into custody originally by the police because of some behavior problem. There we have a weak spot in the community, a spot in which the citizen's activity in community planning is very much needed in order that it may be improved. Again and again you will find a man taken to jail when he is really suffering from a disorder, mental or emotional, which needs psychiatric rather than punitive handling.

Of course the patient can point back a little farther to the teacher or to the public-health nurse who visited his home when he was a baby and to many lost opportunities for preventing the beginnings of illness. There are many formalities and routines and papers and reports that the teacher has to go through that really shove the child back into a secondary position rather than the top position that he should hold in the school's efforts.

This is not by any means the full list of the areas to which the patient may point back. It is just a sample; but these areas are all identified with certain professions, and it is difficult for people in those professions to maintain their perspective. As I said before, they get into channels. There are blinders on their eyes and they do not see off to the sides. For that reason it is especially important that the citizen who is not involved in any one of these professions express his views.

How can we arm the citizen to carry that responsibility in the community? I wish I knew the answer and could hand it to you. I don't know just how he could be armed. I know that we can carry on experiments, and we must try constantly to work out answers. In Monmouth County in New Jersey, where I live, we are trying out one citizen-community approach. Whether it will be the answer or not remains to be seen.

The Mental Hygiene Society has been set up there on the principle that everybody who belongs to it must be on a committee. I said before that the legislatures would appropriate money if the citizens would back them up. But how do you get an informed citizenry that will wisely influence its legislative bodies? Hardly by talking at it. But probably—and this is what we are banking on—probably by giving citizens a job to do, even if in the beginning it is nothing more than to visit one of these abandoned patients in a hospital. But give them a job to do.

With the aim of giving everybody a job to do, and the principle that everybody who belongs must be on a committee, the Mental Hygiene Society has set up some twenty or twenty-five committees. Each member is put on the committee that represents some aspect of mental health in which he has interest.

It is, of course, important to deal with those committees and their members realistically. It has to be recognized that they cannot be treated as if they were

X. *Citizen — Community*

a paid staff and given a big job. Some can be rated in terms of working half an hour a week, some an hour, some up to even ten or fifteen hours a week. But the job has to be cut out according to what committee members can comfortably do, or else they are going to fall down on the job, become discouraged, and get out.

Each one of these committees has something to do. There are many suggestions. They make up their own programs. Each program develops and broadens as it moves along. For instance, there is a Committee on Mental Hygiene in the Schools. What will a group of citizens do in that respect? Someone might say: "We are not authorities on schools, we don't know anything about education." But you vote every time it is necessary to elect a school board, and you make decisions of that kind anyway. It isn't as if you had not made decisions previously—about police, about schools, about hospitals. Decisions are being made all the time. There is a better way to make them that does not entail technical responsibilities of a specialized sort, a way in which each citizen could help.

The Committee on Schools decides on the first thing it will do: each member will attend a school-board meeting. When you canvass people, you find that though a school-board meeting is a public meeting occurring once a month, a very small percentage of the population ever attends. So the Committee on Schools as a start attends a school-board meeting.

The next job is to go to the school superintendent and say: "We have a committee of five people who are interested and are on the Committee on Mental Hygiene in School Work. We know you are interested in that same thing. What is it we can do to help you out? What are the things you had dreamed of getting done in your school system that have been blocked?" And "We know you realize that the children in this school represent all degrees of intelligence, different family backgrounds, and so on. We know you want to make your school meet these different individual needs and do the best possible job. Now, what are the facilities that you have to work with? What are the things you would like to have?"

We know that the members of the Committee on Police Work are not going to find anything to start with, but they ask: "What are the things that are done with the policeman during his period of indoctrination? Have you taken advantage of the fact that Marlborough State Hospital is only ten miles away and you can get some of the staff there to give him a little preparation so that he will know when he runs into a mental problem and will have some idea of what to do about it?"

And the Committee on Mental Hygiene in Old Age says: "These twenty-nine hundred and fifty patients in your hospital are to a great extent old people. What can we do for old people that will relieve the hospital of this responsibility?" Many of the old people who are in state hospitals are not psychotic in the ordinary sense. But their tendency toward forgetfulness creates hazards, and the consequent problems are sometimes solved by hospital commitment. The committee may find new ways of helping.

And so it goes. Committee after committee is attempting to work out some parts of the total complex community problem.

X. Citizen — Community

I think we can say that helps. No one of these five hundred people who now belong to this organization could do a great deal by himself, but he feels support, he feels that he can get other ideas and a strengthening of his position by working with others. Organization is one of the things that can help a citizen relate himself more effectively to his community.

Whatever approaches the citizen or group of citizens makes to these community problems, there always will be problems confronting us. Though some solutions may be effective temporarily, at some points conditions in a democracy are so constantly changing that this year's seeming solution may next year not meet the then current problem. We are driven to do something about certain problems in the community because they touch our hearts deeply—so we respond effectively in the care of children, the crippled, the blind. We are driven by fear and anxiety to undertake programs of protection against or preparation for World War III. We tend, however, to give secondary priorities to human-betterment programs, which are just as truly part of our citizen-community concerns but do not so painfully impinge on our collective consciousness. What we do voluntarily, thoughtfully, and responsibly for protecting and restoring mental health in our community may be considered a most effective yardstick of our citizenship. We citizens are the government in a democracy. Our community in all its strengths and weaknesses will be only what we are willing to make it be.

1. Which states aside from New York are doing a good job in the treatment of the mentally ill?

I wish I had with me the Federal report on the appropriations, state by state, for the mentally ill. I think that would answer your question. They run from something less than one dollar a day—and everyone that has had experience with hospitalization in a general hospital knows what percentage of service that is—up to, I think, in the latest I have seen, around 1946, perhaps six hundred or six hundred and fifty dollars a year, or around two dollars a day.

Now, which states aside from New York are doing a good job? Is any state doing a good job on two dollars a day? The two dollars a day include food, clothes, heat, light, doctors, the nurses—everything.

As states that are doing as good a job as New York we might put Massachusetts and New Jersey and three or four other states in a class in which the best work in the country is being done. And Delaware. But I am not satisfied, in saying that, to imply that any of them is doing the best possible job.

We know perfectly well that the states' emphasis is primarily on the ward and not on sick people in their communities. Otherwise we should not be talking so much about hospitals. We should be talking about Kingston or Yonkers or Queensborough, or something of that sort. Most states have a very long way to go to shift the emphasis from the hospital ward to the community, where the case begins, and we need some real experiments in carrying that through.

X. *Citizen — Community* [273]

2. What do you mean by saying that the neurotic's disturbance is as severe as if he were in a hospital?

I mean that if we take as a measure of values in life the satisfactions that one gets—one's productivity, the good relations between oneself and other people—we also have a measure of mental health. By this measure the neurotic is often just as handicapped as the psychotic. If he can't work, his productivity is zero. He certainly is not a very happy person, and his relationships often break down seriously, so that a person with a very severe neurosis sometimes actually has to be committed to a mental hospital. But that is unusual, and an effort is made to keep him in the community, to which, if his problems are to be solved, he must make some permanent adjustment.

3. Why is there so much money spent in preparing for World War III and not enough for mental hospitals?

Perhaps the question might be broadened to include other things than World War III. It is often said that it is well enough to describe all the fine things that a state ought to be doing, but what is Mississippi going to do? Well, when you take any one of the states and find that the expenditures for cosmetics exceed those for state hospitals, or that the expenditures for cigarettes exceed those for the state hospitals, it becomes a matter of values, and one has to make a decision between them.

If one wants World War III, I suppose that is the reason; or if one wants to safeguard oneself against

World War III, whichever way you put it, it explains why the expenditures are there.

I don't know of any other way to put it.

4. How can we change the present attitudes of the family?

That is one of the big problems. Again and again a patient is, let us say, eighty per cent recovered, and twenty per cent of the lack of recovery could be cared for if the family were so set up as to take him back and give him that care. But the family has become adjusted to having four instead of five people in it. Maybe it has moved into quarters that are good for four but not for five. Maybe other adjustments have come about. Maybe there were some antipathies that were built up at the time or before the time of breakdown.

There are a lot of things that enter in there which require very careful work on the part of the hospital, and that is the job of the social service of the hospital. Unless we provide the hospital with competent social workers, we just have to muddle along, hoping that the family will maintain relations and visit and not abandon the patient.

5. Is there a way of avoiding decentralization of social service when all trends of activity seem to stress centralization?

I think one has to think through to one's concept of community function. My own is—and

X. *Citizen — Community*

someone else may have a different one—that the agencies or divisions of labor in a community are basically worked out along the lines of technical specialization. On the other hand we have omnibus agencies that try to include in themselves all of the technical functions that they may need for their work.

Now, if we think of the divisions of labor as made along technical lines,—one for health, another for education, another for protection, and so on—then the functions of a community are centralized. They are centralized administratively, and they are located in one headquarters. But when it comes time to issue those services, let's give them at the point at which they are of the greatest value to the person being served; not necessarily making him come to the headquarters, but having the staff member sit with the schools or sit with the court or sit with the other agency that needs these technical services.

As a matter of fact, what we do today is to make the bewildered client pick out the various technical services he needs and then put them together himself —when we cannot even do it ourselves. When we have not been able to co-ordinate them, we leave it to him to do it, and he is already bewildered.

So I think the process is one of administrative centralization, but of decentralizing it functionally. The client then does not have to run around and get all these bits and put them together, but is helped locally by those services he needs.

6. Why are old people treated with indifference by the medical profession?

One of the problems of having so many old people in the mental hospitals is that they are thought of as just biding time there. They are, you might say, padding the rolls of the hospital. They are not the special concern of someone who says: "Well now, this is my challenge. This is my patient, and I'm going to try to work something out here."

Possibly if there were special facilities even connected with the hospital which were devoted to the problems of aging, we might learn a lot.

I think we have cut ourselves off from some progress by mixing old people in with the other types of cases. I know that there is at present under way a serious consideration of this problem by one large source of funds devoting its money to the field of the aging. At one state hospital that I am acquainted with where a monthly report is made on the deaths, I know that in September there were eighteen deaths, of which sixteen were due to arteriosclerosis and related problems. In other words, they were deaths due to old age. That gives you something of the size of the problem. One month when there were about twenty-five deaths, five of them were of patients over ninety years of age.

The study of old age has not achieved the degree of interest that pediatrics has, but I think it will come.

X. Citizen — Community

7. Has mental health increased? Do we just recognize more cases?

I think there is no way I can judge whether mental health has increased. Certainly, as with the community, a solution that holds a person stable today does not serve tomorrow; and the problems that we encounter today, amid the complexities that we face, may break down one individual of the same degree of mental stability as another who would not break down under similar circumstances. But certainly we do have much better facilities for detection of cases.

The increases that we see in statistics I believe for the most part are due to better detection and are not evidence of greater ill health.

8. What shall a teacher do when she encounters the problem of mental ill health and wants to help her students?

I have a feeling that the best thing she can do is to be the best possible teacher, first of all, and not feel compelled to step outside of her job and try to do something in the way of technical help in a field in which she isn't prepared.

9. Have you knowledge of other community efforts of the kind in Monmouth County?

It is an experiment there, as I say; whether it will work or not, nobody knows. We will try to make it work. We shall change it a good deal before it will work, probably. I don't know of anything of exactly that sort, but I do know that the involvement of people in committee work is an old idea. This is merely borrowing that idea.

There was a time when the New Jersey State Conference of Social Work followed that principle, once a year. Instead of having a lot of papers, they just had a keynote speech, and then divided the whole group up into committees A to Z and gave each committee the chance to sit down and discuss the keynote speech.

This is somewhat the same principle as involving people in a practical job, and out of it they learn much in addition to doing some valuable things themselves.

10. How can that sort of thing be done in New York?

New York is one of the most difficult cities to do things of that sort in, yet there have been neighborhood activities in New York and in Chicago, too, in which groups of citizens have got together and done really valuable things. But it is more difficult in a city of this size.

RENEWALS 458-4574

DATE DUE			
FEB 1 1			
GAYLORD			PRINTED IN U.S.A